European Computer Driving Licence®

ECDL Advanced

Syllabus 2.0

Module AM5 - Database

Using Microsoft® Access 2003

Release ECDL230v1

Published by:

> CiA Training Ltd
> Business & Innovation Centre
> Sunderland Enterprise Park
> Sunderland SR5 2TA
> United Kingdom
>
> Tel: +44 (0) 191 549 5002
> Fax: +44 (0) 191 549 9005
>
> E-mail: info@ciatraining.co.uk
> Web: www.ciatraining.co.uk
>
> **ISBN-13: 978 1 86005 655 0**

This training, which has been approved by ECDL Foundation, includes exercise items intended to assist Candidates in their training for an ECDL Certification Programme. These exercises are not ECDL Foundation certification tests. For information about authorised Test Centres in different national territories, please refer to the ECDL Foundation website at www.ecdl.org

First published 2009

Copyright © 2009 CiA Training Ltd

All rights reserved. No part of this publication may be reproduced, stored in a retrieval system, or transmitted in any form or by any means (electronic, mechanical, photocopying, recording or otherwise) without the prior written permission of CiA Training Limited.

Microsoft is a registered trademark and Windows is a trademark of the Microsoft Corporation. Screen images reproduced by permission of the Microsoft Corporation. All other trademarks in this book are acknowledged as the property of their respective owners.

European Computer Driving Licence, ECDL, International Computer Driving Licence, ICDL, e-Citizen and related logos are all registered Trade Marks of The European Computer Driving Licence Foundation Limited ("ECDL Foundation").

CiA Training Ltd is an entity independent of ECDL Foundation and is not associated with ECDL Foundation in any manner. This courseware may be used to assist candidates to prepare for the ECDL Foundation Certification Programme as titled on the courseware. Neither ECDL Foundation nor **CiA Training Ltd** warrants that the use of this courseware publication will ensure passing of the tests for that ECDL Foundation Certification Programme. This courseware publication has been independently reviewed and approved by ECDL Foundation as covering the learning objectives for the ECDL Foundation Certification Programme.

Confirmation of this approval can be obtained by reviewing the Partners Page in the About Us Section of the website www.ecdl.org

The material contained in this courseware publication has not been reviewed for technical accuracy and does not guarantee that candidates will pass the test for the ECDL Foundation Certification Programme. Any and all assessment items and/or performance-based exercises contained in this courseware relate solely to this publication and do not constitute or imply certification by ECDL Foundation in respect of the ECDL Foundation Certification Programme or any other ECDL Foundation test. Irrespective of how the material contained in this courseware is deployed, for example in a learning management system (LMS) or a customised interface, nothing should suggest to the candidate that this material constitutes certification or can lead to certification through any other process than official ECDL Foundation certification testing.

For details on sitting a test for an ECDL Foundation certification programme, please contact your country's designated National Licensee or visit the ECDL Foundation's website at www.ecdl.org.

Candidates using this courseware must be registered with the National Operator before undertaking a test for an ECDL Foundation Certification Programme. Without a valid registration, the test(s) cannot be undertaken and no certificate, nor any other form of recognition, can be given to a candidate.
Registration should be undertaken with your country's designated National Licensee at an Approved Test Centre.

ECDL/ICDL Module AM5 - Database Advanced Level

Downloading the Data Files

The data associated with these exercises must be downloaded from our website. Go to: **www.ciatraining.co.uk/data**. Follow the on screen instructions to download the appropriate data files.

By default, the data files will be downloaded to **My Documents\CIA DATA FILES\Advanced ECDL\AM5 Access 2003 Data**.

If you prefer, the data can be supplied on CD at an additional cost. Contact the Sales team at *info@ciatraining.co.uk*.

Aims

To demonstrate the ability to use a database application on a personal computer.

To understand and accomplish more advanced operations associated with database design.

To demonstrate some of the more advanced features including field properties, relationships, joins, action queries and macros.

Objectives

After completing the guide the user will be able to:

- Create databases
- Use Lookup fields
- Set field properties
- Perform advanced queries
- Create and amend relationships and joins
- Create forms and form controls
- Create reports and grouped reports
- Import and link data
- Create action queries
- Create and run macros.

Assessment of Knowledge

At the end of this guide is a section called the **Record of Achievement Matrix**. Before the guide is started it is recommended that the user completes the matrix to measure the level of current knowledge.

Tick boxes are provided for each feature. **1** is for no knowledge, **2** some knowledge and **3** is for competent.

After working through a section, complete the matrix for that section and only when competent in all areas move on to the next section.

Contents

SECTION 1 FUNDAMENTALS 8
   1 - DATABASE CONCEPTS 9
   2 - DATABASE DEVELOPMENT 10
   3 - SQL 11
   4 - CREATING A DATABASE 12
   5 - CREATING TABLES 13
   6 - REVISION 15

SECTION 2 FIELD PROPERTIES 16
   7 - LOOKUP FIELDS 17
   8 - LOOKUP A TABLE 19
   9 - DEFAULT VALUES 20
   10 - SETTING A MANDATORY FIELD 21
   11 - VALIDATION RULES/TEXT 23
   12 - INPUT MASKS 25
   13 - REVISION 28

SECTION 3 QUERIES 29
   14 - SUM 30
   15 - COUNT 31
   16 - AVERAGE VALUES 32
   17 - MAXIMUM AND MINIMUM VALUES 33
   18 - CALCULATED FIELDS: QUERIES 34
   19 - PARAMETER QUERIES 36
   20 - USING WILDCARDS IN A QUERY 38
   21 - REVISION 39
   22 - REVISION 40

SECTION 4 RELATIONSHIPS 41
   23 - APPLYING A PRIMARY KEY 42
   24 - APPLYING RELATIONSHIPS 44
   25 - ONE-TO-ONE RELATIONSHIPS 47
   26 - MANY-TO-MANY RELATIONSHIPS 49
   27 - APPLYING JOINS 51
   28 - SELF JOINS 53
   29 - REFERENTIAL INTEGRITY 55
   30 - CASCADE OPTIONS 57
   31 - REVISION 59
   32 - REVISION 60

SECTION 5 FORMS 61
   33 - MAIN/SUBFORM: FORM WIZARD 62
   34 - MAIN/SUBFORM: SUBFORM WIZARD 64
   35 - MAIN/SUBFORM: MANUAL 66
   36 - LINKING FORMS 68
   37 - REVISION 70
   38 - REVISION 71

SECTION 6 FORM CONTROLS 72

- 39 - CALCULATED FIELDS: FORMS 73
- 40 - COMBO BOX 1: WIZARD 75
- 41 - LIMIT TO LIST 78
- 42 - COMBO BOX 2: WIZARD 79
- 43 - COMBO BOX 3: WIZARD 80
- 44 - COMBO BOX: MANUAL 81
- 45 - LIST BOXES 83
- 46 - CHECK BOXES 85
- 47 - OPTION GROUPS 86
- 48 - FORM HEADERS AND FOOTERS 88
- 49 - COMMAND BUTTON: WIZARD 89
- 50 - REVISION 90
- 51 - REVISION 91

SECTION 7 REPORTS 92

- 52 - GROUPED REPORT: WIZARD 93
- 53 - GROUPED REPORT: MANUAL 95
- 54 - SUBREPORTS 97
- 55 - CALCULATED FIELDS: REPORTS 99
- 56 - CALCULATING PERCENTAGES 102
- 57 - REPORT HEADERS & FOOTERS 103
- 58 - PRINTING REPORTS 105
- 59 - REVISION 106
- 60 - REVISION 107

SECTION 8 IMPORT AND LINK DATA 108

- 61 - IMPORTING SPREADSHEETS 109
- 62 - IMPORTING TEXT FILES 111
- 63 - IMPORTING TABLES 113
- 64 - LINKING DATA 114
- 65 - REVISION 116
- 66 - REVISION 117

SECTION 9 ACTION QUERIES 118

- 67 - APPEND QUERY 119
- 68 - DELETE QUERY 121
- 69 - MAKE-TABLE QUERY 122
- 70 - UPDATE QUERY 124
- 71 - REVISION 125
- 72 - REVISION 126

SECTION 10 QUERY WIZARDS 127

- 73 - CROSSTAB QUERY 128
- 74 - FIND DUPLICATES QUERY 130
- 75 - FIND UNMATCHED QUERY 131
- 76 - REVISION 132

SECTION 11 MACROS 133
- 77 - Create a New Macro 134
- 78 - Attaching a Macro to a Control 136
- 79 - Attaching a Macro to an Object 138
- 80 - Create Macros from Controls 139
- 81 - Command Button Macros 141
- 82 - Revision 142
- 83 - Revision 143

ANSWERS 144

GLOSSARY 146

INDEX 147

RECORD OF ACHIEVEMENT MATRIX 149

OTHER PRODUCTS FROM CIA TRAINING LTD 152

Section 1
Fundamentals

By the end of this Section you should be able to:

> **Understand Database Concepts**
>
> **Understand SQL**
>
> **Create a Database**
>
> **Design a Table**

To gain an understanding of the above features, work through the **Driving Lessons** in this **Section**.

For each **Driving Lesson**, read the **Park and Read** instructions, without touching the keyboard, then work through the numbered steps of the **Manoeuvres** on the computer. Complete the **Revision Exercise(s)** at the end of the section to test your knowledge.

Driving Lesson 1 - Database Concepts

Park and Read

Applications for Databases

Databases are used to maintain and retrieve data in various ways; they can certainly help to make an organisation more streamlined and efficient. Many companies use database driven **dynamic websites**; this allows them to update prices and product information, maintain online mailing lists and lets their customers search the data, for example. **Website content management systems** allow non-technical users to make changes and are used as a maintenance tool to create and manage web content. Databases can also be designed to be used as **customer relationship management systems**. Information is stored on current and prospective customers; it can be used to improve services to customers by targeted sales and marketing. **Enterprise resource planning databases** contain data for various business functions in an integrated form. For example, they can be used to control manufacturing, logistics, distribution, inventories, shipping and invoicing.

Database Models

The specification describing how a database is structured and used is known as a **database model**. The main models are:

> **hierarchical** - one of the first models to be widely accepted and used. Records contain groups of parent/child relationships, similar to a tree structure. This model is fast and simple to use, but inflexible because it only contains one-to-many relationships.
>
> **relational** - data is organised logically in a set of related tables. It can be accessed or reassembled in many different ways without having to reorganise the database tables. A relational database is relatively easy to create and access and is easy to add to.
>
> **object-oriented** - data is represented by objects. These models do not all support SQL (see DL 3) and so have their limitations.

Manoeuvres

1. If you have an active internet connection, start your browser application and view the web site **www.ciatraining.co.uk**.

2. Use the links to search for information on any product, **ECDL Advanced** for example. All the information that is presented (icons, description, content, etc.) is held on a dynamic database. As we release new materials, the database is updated and the information is automatically available immediately to users of our web site.

3. Close the site and your browser.

Driving Lesson 2 - Database Development

▣ Park and Read

There are various stages in the "life cycle" of a database.

Logical Design

The first and most important stage is the design, which has to be logical and take into account everything that the database is to be used for; possible future development should also be considered. One way to design a database system is to define the output that is required from the system, then design the various components to achieve that result.

Database Creation

Next is the database creation - the setting up of tables, relationships, forms for data input, query and report definitions. This requires good technical knowledge of a database application.

Data Entry

Once the basic structure has been created, the starting data must be input. This can be a very long process if it has to be done manually, but there are options to import data from other applications.

Data Maintenance

Once the database is running it must be managed. A database is only useful if the integrity of the data is maintained. New information must be added and obsolete data removed promptly. In a large database, a database administrator may be required to do this task.

Information Retrieval

The database can then be interrogated and information retrieved via queries, forms and reports. Sometimes users are restricted to using only the components that are provided, sometimes they will be allowed to build their own queries, reports, etc.

In a large organisation there may be different people for each of the stages above. In a small organisation, one person may have to do it all.

Access 2003   ECDL/ICDL   Section 1 Fundamentals

Driving Lesson 3 - SQL

Park and Read

When a query is created in *Access*, the application converts this into a program in a language called **SQL**, **Structured Query Language**. This language is very widely used across many computing platforms and can be used to write systems in its own right. There is no need for the average user to ever deal with the SQL code behind queries, but it is useful to know about it.

Manoeuvres

1. Start *Access* and open the **Supermarket** database.

2. Select **Queries** from the **Objects** bar in the **Database Window**.

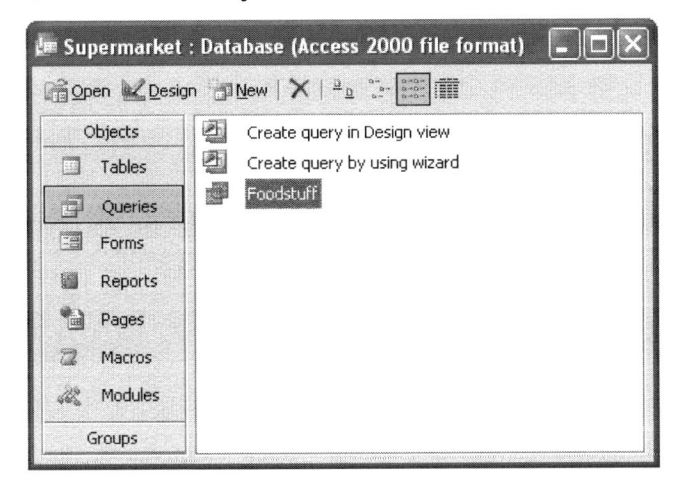

3. Double click **Foodstuff** to run the query then click the design icon to see the design criteria. The query selects records with a category of **Foodstuffs** from the **Stock** table and displays the fields **Product Ref.**, **Item** and **Category**.

4. Select **View | SQL View**. The **SQL** code for the query is displayed.

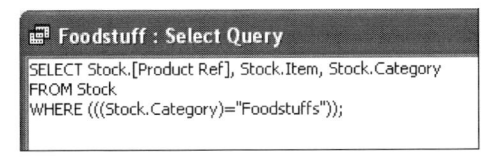

    ```
    SELECT Stock.[Product Ref], Stock.Item, Stock.Category
    FROM Stock
    WHERE (((Stock.Category)="Foodstuffs"));
    ```

5. Click the **Close** button, to close the **SQL** view.

6. Close the database.

Section 1 Fundamentals   ECDL/ICDL   Access 2003

Driving Lesson 4 - Creating a Database

Park and Read

The following Driving Lessons demonstrate how to create a database from scratch. In this example an **Antiquities** database will record sales of ancient artefacts.

Manoeuvres

1. From a blank *Access* screen click the **New** button, ▢, from the toolbar to open the **New File** task pane.

2. Select **Blank Database** from the **New** section of the **Task Pane**.

3. In the **Save in** box, select the folder where the database is to be saved (see page 4 - **Downloading the Data Files** for the location).

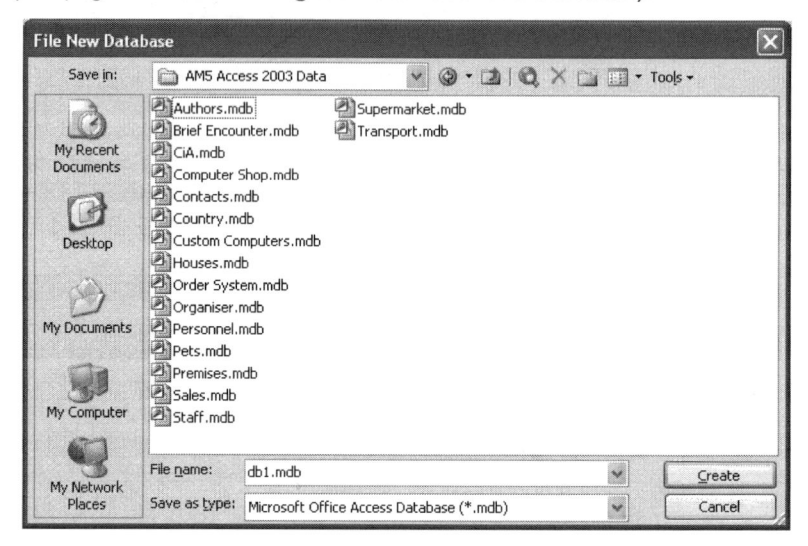

4. In the **File name** box, type **Antiquities** and click **Create**.

5. The new **Database Window** is now visible with the database name in the **Title Bar** at the top.

> Notice that the default format for a database created in Access 2003 is Access 2000 format. This means the new database will be compatible with either the 2000, XP or 2003 versions of Access.

6. Leave the database open.

Access 2003 *ECDL/ICDL* *Section 1 Fundamentals*

Driving Lesson 5 - Creating Tables

Park and Read

Tables can be created using a wizard. A wizard gives step by step instructions for the initial setting up and applies default formatting, such as date formats and number formats. Alternatively a table can be created in **Design View** which allows a free hand for formatting.

Manoeuvres

1. Select the **Tables** object from the **Database Window**, and click the **New** button.

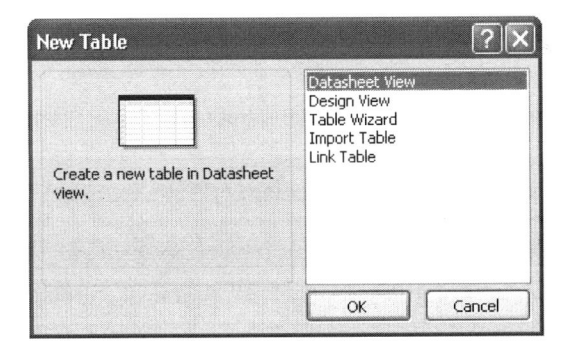

2. Choose **Design View** from the **New Table** dialog box and click **OK**. The table design window is displayed.

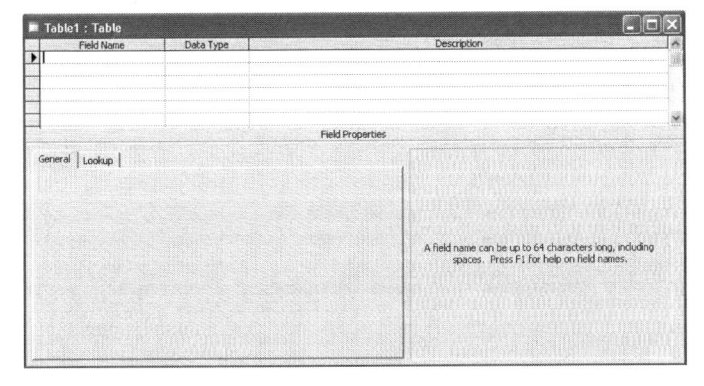

*You can also double click the shortcut, Create table in Design view, in the **Database Window**.*

3. In the first **Field Name** row, enter **Artefact**.

Module AM5 Database Advanced Level   13   © *CiA Training Ltd 2009*

Section 1 Fundamentals　　　　ECDL/ICDL　　　　Access 2003

Driving Lesson 5 - Continued

4. Press **<Tab>** to move to the next column. **Text** appears in the **Data Type** column. Press **<Tab>**.

5. The cursor is now in the **Description** column; this column is optional. Enter **Type of Artefact** into this column, then press **<Tab>**.

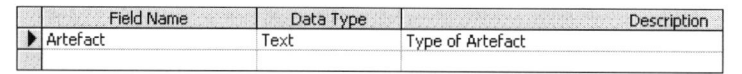

Field Name	Data Type	Description
Artefact	Text	Type of Artefact

6. For the next **Field Name**, enter **Date Sold** and press **<Tab>**.

7. Click on the drop down list in the **Data Type** field and select **Date/Time** from the selection.

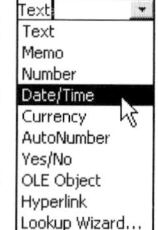

8. Press **<Tab>** to move into the **Description** column and type **Date the artefact was sold** then press **<Tab>** again.

9. Enter **Price** as the third field name, **<Tab>**, then select **Currency** as the **Data Type** and enter **Selling price** as the description.

10. The next **Field Name** is **Quantity Sold**, the **Data Type** is **Number** and the **Description** is **Number of artefacts sold**.

11. For the next field enter **Information**, the **Data Type** is **Memo** and the **Description** is **History and identifying features**.

[i] **Memo** is used when the field is likely to contain more than 255 characters, which is the maximum allowed by **Text**.

12. For the final field, enter the name **Web Address**, the **Data Type** **Hyperlink** and a **Description** of **Related web site?**

13. Save the table by clicking on the **Save** button. Name the table **Artefact Sales**.

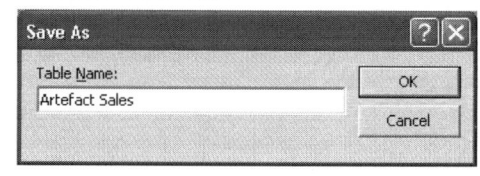

14. Click **OK**.

15. A message is displayed regarding **Primary Keys**. Click on **No** to save the table without creating a primary key.

16. It is now possible to specify certain formatting options for each field. These are selected in the **Field Properties** area. Basic **Field Properties** were covered at standard ECDL level, some more advanced options are covered in the next section.

17. Close the database.

Access 2003 ECDL/ICDL Section 1 Fundamentals

Driving Lesson 6 - Revision

This is not an ECDL test. Testing may only be carried out through certified ECDL test centres. This covers the features introduced in this section. Try not to refer to the preceding Driving Lessons while completing it.

1. Create a new database named **Stock** and create the following fields in **Design View**:

Field Name	Data Type	Field Size/Format
Ref	Number	Long Integer
Item	Text	30
Bought by	Text	30
Supplier	Text	2
Price	Currency	
Last Ordered	Date/Time	Short Date
Stock	Number	Long Integer

2. Save the table as **Stationery**, without defining a **Primary Key**.

3. Close the table, saving the design.

4. Close the database.

5. Open the database **Order System**.

6. Click the **Relationships** button, on the main toolbar to see how the four tables are related. Close the **Relationships** window.

7. Open the query **Example1** in **Design** view. The data in this query comes from how many different tables?

8. Run the query. The data is presented in a single list, regardless of the fact that it is from different tables. Close the query and the database.

See the **Answers** section at the back of the guide.

If you experienced any difficulty completing the Revision, refer back to the Driving Lessons in this section. Then redo the Revision.

Once you are confident with the features, complete the Record of Achievement Matrix referring to the section at the end of the guide. Only when competent move on to the next Section.

Section 2
Field Properties

By the end of this Section you should be able to:

> **Create Lookup Fields**
>
> **Set and Modify Default Values**
>
> **Set Mandatory Fields**
>
> **Create Validation Rules and Text**
>
> **Create Input Masks**

To gain an understanding of the above features, work through the **Driving Lessons** in this **Section**.

For each **Driving Lesson**, read the **Park and Read** instructions, without touching the keyboard, then work through the numbered steps of the **Manoeuvres** on the computer. Complete the **Revision Exercise(s)** at the end of the section to test your knowledge.

Access 2003   ECDL/ICDL   *Section 2 Field Properties*

Driving Lesson 7 - Lookup Fields

Park and Read

When creating a table, a field can be defined that displays a list of possible entries. This is called a **Lookup Field** and will speed up data input and reduce typing mistakes, because at data entry time there is no need to enter any values, merely select an entry from the presented list. The field can also be set so that only those entries in the **Lookup Field** list will be accepted.

There are two options: either the possible values for the field will be manually typed into the field definition, or the field will lookup its possible values from another table in the database. The first option is covered in this lesson, and is used when there are not many values to choose from and they are not expected to change very often.

Manoeuvres

1. Open the **Custom Computers** database. Open the **Repairs** table in **Design View**. A new lookup field is to be created, called **Processed By**.

2. Position the cursor under **Date**. Enter the **Field Name** as **Processed By** and from **Data Type** choose **Lookup Wizard**. After a few seconds the **Lookup Wizard** appears.

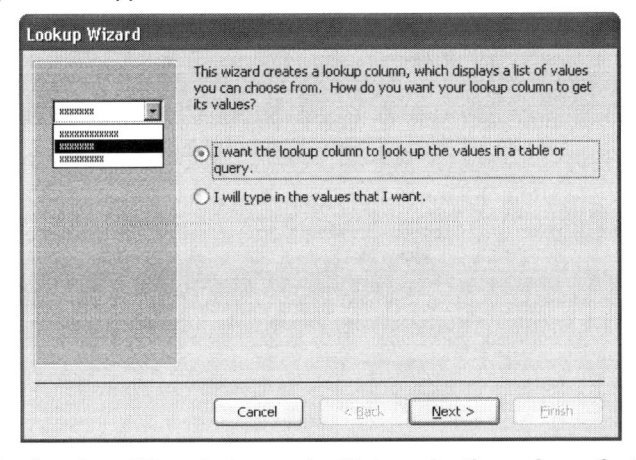

3. From the **Lookup Wizard** choose **I will type in the values that I want** and click **Next**.

4. Specify the **Number of columns**: as **1** and enter the following values into **Col 1**, separating each entry using the **<Tab>** key: **Davison**, **Jones**, **Hussan** and **Peters**.

Module AM5 Database Advanced Level   17   © *CiA Training Ltd 2009*

Section 2 Field Properties   ECDL/ICDL   Access 2003

Driving Lesson 7 - Continued

5. Click **Next**. The label **Processed By** is correct. Click **Finish** to create the **Lookup Field**.

6. Save the table and switch to **Datasheet View**. The new field is displayed.

7. **Davidson** processed **Job No 1**. Click in **Processed By** for **Job No 1**.

8. Click on the down arrow and choose **Davison** from the list.

9. Click in **Processed By** for **Job No 2** and enter the single character **H**. **Hussan** appears in **Processed By** for **Job No 2**.

10. Switch to **Design View**. In **Field Properties**, select the **Lookup** tab.

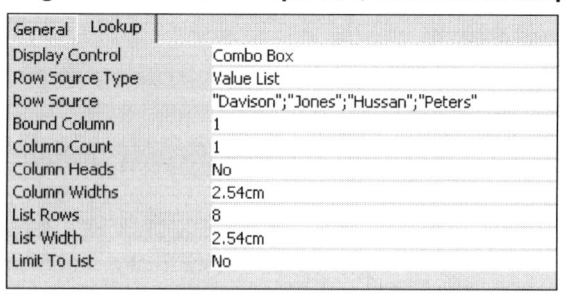

General Lookup	
Display Control	Combo Box
Row Source Type	Value List
Row Source	"Davison";"Jones";"Hussan";"Peters"
Bound Column	1
Column Count	1
Column Heads	No
Column Widths	2.54cm
List Rows	8
List Width	2.54cm
Limit To List	No

11. **Row Source** shows the entries that appear in the field and these can be amended here. **Peters** leaves the company and is replaced by **Cowell**. Highlight the text **Peters** and type **Cowell**.

12. Change the **Limit To List** option to **Yes**. Save the changes to the table and then switch back to **Datasheet View**.

13. Try and enter the name **Chapman** in the **Processed By** field of one of the records. A message will appear.

> Microsoft Office Access
> The text you entered isn't an item in the list.
> Select an item from the list, or enter text that matches one of the listed items.
> OK

14. Because **Limit To List** is set, only the names in the **Lookup** field list box will be accepted. Click **OK** and then select from the list of possible names.

15. Switch to **Design View**, click in the **Processed By** field and select the **Lookup** tab in **Field Properties**.

16. Click the drop down arrow in the **Display Control** field and select **Text Box**. The field is no longer a lookup field.

17. Save the table and leave it open for the next Driving Lesson.

Access 2003   *ECDL/ICDL*   *Section 2 Field Properties*

Driving Lesson 8 - Lookup a Table

Park and Read

It is also possible for a **Lookup Field** to look up values from a different table in the database. This can be useful to maintain integrity between tables. For example a table of customer orders may contain a customer field. If this is made a lookup field to the **Customer** table, orders can only be entered for customer already on the **Customer** table.

Manoeuvres

1. Display the **Repairs** table in **Design View**. The **Engineer** field is to be changed to a **Lookup** field.

2. Click in the **Engineer** field and from **Data Type** choose **Lookup Wizard**.

3. This time choose the option **I want the lookup column to look up the values in a table or query**. Click **Next**.

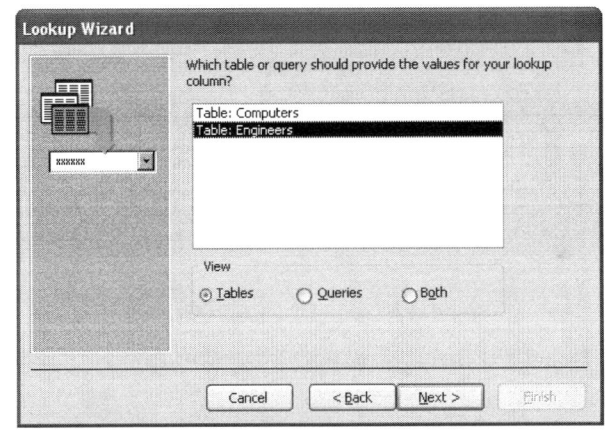

4. Select the **Engineers** table and click **Next**.

5. Select **Engineer Name** from the left and click [>] to select it. Click **Next**.

6. Select **Engineer Name**, **Ascending** as the sort order, click **Next**.

7. The column width should be acceptable, click **Next**.

8. The label **Engineer** is correct. Click **Finish** to create the **Lookup Field**. You will be prompted to save the table. Click **Yes**.

9. Switch to **Datasheet View**, click in any **Engineer** field and click the drop down arrow. Only the names from the **Engineers** table will be available.

10. Close the table and the database.

Driving Lesson 9 - Default Values

Park and Read

A **Default Value** is a value that is automatically entered into a particular field of every new record. When records are added, the default value can either be accepted or changed.

The default value is entered in the **Field Properties** area when in **Design View**, in the **Default Value** box.

Manoeuvres

1. In the **CiA** database, open the **Order Details** table in **Design View**.

2. Select the **Amount** field and position the cursor in the **Default Value** field property.

3. Enter **1**. Every new record will now automatically appear with the number 1 already inserted in the field. This value can be overwritten if necessary.

4. Save the table and switch to **Datasheet View**. Start a new record.

5. Enter the following details:

Order Ref	Product Ref	Line Number	Amount
225	TA1	1	

6. **1** should automatically be in the **Amount** field. This is the correct figure for this record so close the table.

7. Open the **Orders** table in **Design View**.

8. Select the **Order Date** field and in the **Default Value** enter **=Date()**. This will automatically show the current date for the next new record.

9. Set the **Paid** field **Default Value** to **No**. Save the changes and switch to **Datasheet View** and view the new record row at the bottom of the table.

10. Notice how today's date is in **Order Date** and **Paid** shows **No**.

11. Close the table then open the **Order Details** table in **Design View**.

12. Change the default value for **Amount** to **2**, save the table and switch to **Datasheet View**.

13. View the new record row and notice how **Amount** shows the modified default value.

14. Close the table but leave the database open.

Driving Lesson 10 - Setting a Mandatory Field

▣ Park and Read

Some fields in a database will be essential to maintain the usefulness of the system. For these fields, it is possible to set field properties so that the field is mandatory or required, i.e. it <u>must</u> be completed. It will then be impossible to enter a record without data in this field.

Manoeuvres

1. Using the **CiA** database, open the **Customer Details** table in **Design View**.

2. To ensure rapid contact with all customers, the **Telephone** number is to be made a mandatory field. Select the **Field Name** for **Telephone**.

3. Click at the far right of the **Required** field property. The default value for this property is **No**. This means that a record can be added to the table without an entry in this field.

4. Select **Yes** from the drop down list. Now any record added to the table <u>must</u> have an entry in this field, or the addition will not be accepted.

5. Save the table. As a new rule has been defined, any data which is currently in the table may not now be valid. The following message will appear:

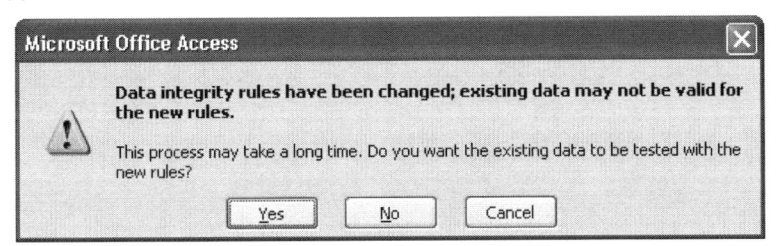

6. There are three options. **Yes** will test the existing data with the new rule. **No** will not test the existing data but will apply the validation to all new records. **Cancel** will return to the **Design View**. Select **Yes**.

7. Testing will start and because there is an existing record on the table which does not match the rule, i.e. without a telephone number, a dialog box will appear giving three options.

Driving Lesson 10 - Continued

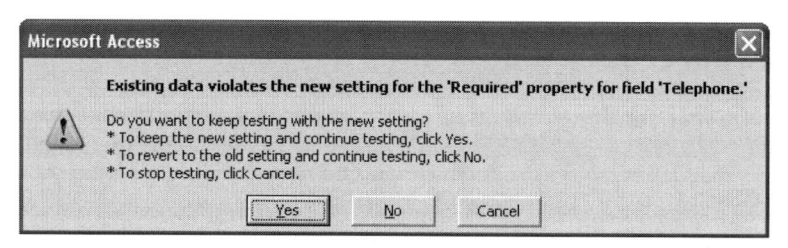

> **Microsoft Access**
>
> Existing data violates the new setting for the 'Required' property for field 'Telephone.'
> Do you want to keep testing with the new setting?
> * To keep the new setting and continue testing, click Yes.
> * To revert to the old setting and continue testing, click No.
> * To stop testing, click Cancel.
>
> [Yes]   [No]   [Cancel]

8. Read the options, then click **Yes** to retain the new settings and continue the testing.

9. Switch to **Datasheet View**.

10. Enter a telephone number for **Customer Ref 30**.

11. Start a new record and enter the following details:

    (32), Mr Vikram Singh, Exotic Foods, High Street, Newcastle, NE1 2JG.

12. Press **<Tab>** to leave the **Telephone** field blank.

13. Tab to the end of the record. The following warning appears:

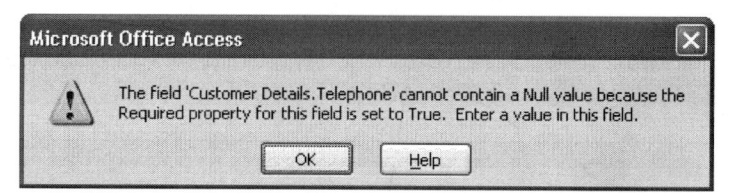

> **Microsoft Office Access**
>
> The field 'Customer Details.Telephone' cannot contain a Null value because the Required property for this field is set to True. Enter a value in this field.
>
> [OK]   [Help]

14. Click **OK** and enter the following telephone number: **0191 2661111**.

15. Leave the table open.

Driving Lesson 11 - Validation Rules/Text

Park and Read

Validation Rules are used to set the requirements of the text that the user enters into a particular field. It defines the only permitted entries that the user may make.

If text which breaks the validation rule is entered, a message displaying some pre-set **Validation Text** will be displayed, as defined by the user.

Validation rules and text are defined in the **Field Properties** when viewing a table in **Design View**.

Manoeuvres

1. View the **Customer Details** table in **Design View**.

2. Select the **Title** field and position the cursor in the **Validation Rule** field property. Enter the following text.

    Mr or Mrs or Miss or Ms or Dr

   This defines the permitted entries for this field. Only these 5 titles will be allowed.

3. In the **Validation Text** property, enter

    The title must be one of the following: Mr, Mrs, Miss, Ms or Dr.

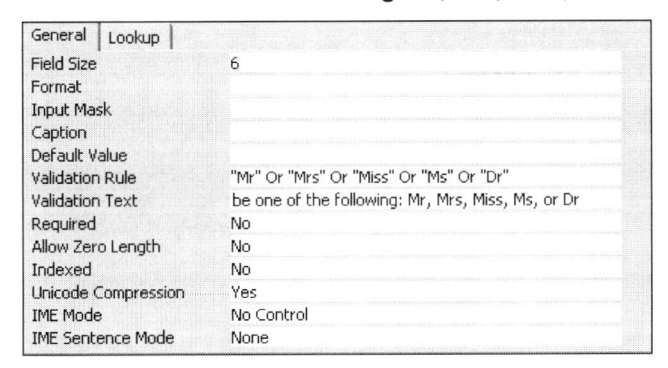

General	Lookup	
Field Size	6	
Format		
Input Mask		
Caption		
Default Value		
Validation Rule	"Mr" Or "Mrs" Or "Miss" Or "Ms" Or "Dr"	
Validation Text	be one of the following: Mr, Mrs, Miss, Ms, or Dr	
Required	No	
Allow Zero Length	No	
Indexed	No	
Unicode Compression	Yes	
IME Mode	No Control	
IME Sentence Mode	None	

   This defines the message that will appear if any text is entered that does not match the list defined in the **Validation Rule**.

4. Save the table. Because the rules for the data have changed, the option for testing the existing data will be displayed.

Driving Lesson 11 - Continued

5. Click **Yes** at the prompt to test the data. There should be no exceptions found.

6. Check in **Datasheet View** and confirm that all the existing data already fits the new validation rule.

7. Start a new record. In the **Title** field enter **Sir**. Press **<Tab>**. The following message appears:

   > Microsoft Office Access
   > The title must be one of the following: Mr, Mrs, Miss, Ms or Dr

8. This is because **Sir** does not match any of the entries in the **Validation Rule**. Click **OK**.

9. Enter **Mr** in the **Title** field. Press **<Tab>**. As **Mr** is one of the values included in the **Validation Rule** it allows this to be entered.

10. Fill in the rest of the record with your own details, changing the **Title** to one of the other allowed values if necessary.

11. To edit the validation rule, switch to **Design View**.

12. Select the **Title** field and click at the end of the **Validation Rule** field property, after **"Dr"**.

13. Type in **Or "Sir"**.

14. Amend the **Validation Text** property to ...**Miss, Ms, Dr or Sir**.

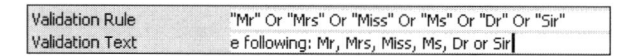

Validation Rule	"Mr" Or "Mrs" Or "Miss" Or "Ms" Or "Dr" Or "Sir"
Validation Text	e following: Mr, Mrs, Miss, Ms, Dr or Sir

15. Save the table, select **Yes** at the prompt and switch to **Datasheet View**.

16. Start a new record and type **Sir** in the **Title** field. Press **<Tab>**. As the validation rule has been edited, **Sir** is now a permitted entry and does not result in an error message.

17. Click the **Undo** button, to cancel this record entry.

18. Leave the table open for the next Driving Lesson.

Driving Lesson 12 - Input Masks

Park and Read

Input Masks control how data is entered and displayed in a field. The **Input Mask** field property in **Design View** is used. A combination of different symbols is entered, which defines the way in which data in that field is expected to be entered, and how it will be shown. The symbols used are:

Mask Character	Used for
0	Number - entry required.
9	Number - entry not required.
#	Number, + or -, or space - entry not required.
L	Letter - entry required.
?	Letter - entry not required.
A	Letter or Number - entry required.
a	Letter or Number - entry not required.
&	Any character or space - entry required.
C	Any character or space - entry not required.
. ,	Decimal point and thousands separators.
: /	Date and time separators.
<	Converts characters to the right to lowercase.
>	Converts characters to the right to uppercase.
!	Mask fills from right to left.
\	Makes the character that follows to be displayed as itself, e.g. \9 will be displayed as 9.

A **Wizard** is available with some preset masks.

Manoeuvres

1. Display the **Customer Details** table in **Design View**.

2. Select the **Telephone** field and click in the **Input Mask** field property.

3. The **Build** button appears . Click on it once to view the **Input Mask Wizard**.

4. Select **Phone Number** from the **Input Mask** box.

Driving Lesson 12 - Continued

5. Click **Next**.
6. Click **Next** on this screen without changing any settings.
7. Choose to store the data **With the symbols in the mask...** and click **Next**.
8. Click **Finish**. The mask appears in the **Telephone** field property. The **9** signifies that a number <u>may</u> be entered at that position, the **0** signifies a number <u>must</u> be entered. Both signify a numeric entry only. The mask characters end at the first semicolon.
9. Save the table and switch to **Datasheet View**. Notice existing data is not checked against the mask. Add any new record entering any details, but leave the **Telephone** field blank. This results in an error message because the field is now **Required**.
10. Try and enter **abc** in the **Telephone** field. This will not be allowed, the entry must be numeric.
11. Type **123** and press **<Enter>**. An error message will be shown, including the format of the appropriate input mask.

Driving Lesson 12 - Continued

> **Microsoft Office Access**
> The value you entered isn't appropriate for the input mask '\(0009") "00090009;0;_' specified for this field.
> OK   Help

12. Click **OK**.

13. Position the cursor immediately after the brackets and type **1234567**. The entry should look like **(123_)1234567**. This fits the mask and should be accepted.

14. The mask can be modified directly in **Field Properties** without using the Wizard. Switch to **Design View** and change the mask to **(0009")"00090009; 0;**. The first three zeros means that at least 3 numbers of an area code <u>must</u> be entered.

15. Save the table and switch to **Datasheet View**. Start a new record, entering any details. A telephone number without an area code will not now be accepted. Enter **(0123) 4567890** and press **<Enter>**.

16. Switch to **Design View**. Select the **Telephone** field and click in the **Input Mask** field property.

17. Click and drag to highlight the entire content of the **Input Mask** field and press **<Delete>**. The **Input Mask** is removed.

18. Close the table, saving at the prompt, and close the database.

Driving Lesson 13 - Revision

This is not an ECDL test. Testing may only be carried out through certified ECDL test centres. This covers the features introduced in this section. Try not to refer to the preceding Driving Lessons while completing it.

1. Open the **Houses** database. Open the **Property** table in **Design View**.

2. Change the **Type of Property** field to be a **Lookup** field with the entries **House**, **Apartment**, **Town House**.

3. For the **Glazing** field, create a **Validation Rule** that will only accept the following values: **None**, **Standard**, **Double**, and **Tinted**.

4. Create **Validation Text** to go with the **Validation Rule**.

5. Set the **Type of Property** and **Glazing** fields to be **Mandatory**.

6. Save the table and close the database.

7. Open the **Premises** database. Open the **Offers** table in **Design View**.

8. Change the **Property Ref** field in the **Offers** table to be a **Lookup** field that will look up possible values from the **Property Ref** field in the **Commercial** table.

9. Use **Limit To List** to ensure this field only accepts one of these entries.

10. Save the table and display it in **Datasheet View**. Add a new record to test the **Lookup** field.

11. Close the table and database.

If you experienced any difficulty completing the Revision, refer back to the Driving Lessons in this section. Then redo the Revision.

Once you are confident with the features, complete the Record of Achievement Matrix referring to the section at the end of the guide. Only when competent move on to the next Section.

Section 3
Queries

By the end of this Section you should be able to:

> Create Sum and Count Queries
>
> Use Group By in Queries
>
> Show Average, Maximum and Minimum Values
>
> Create Calculated Fields
>
> Create Parameter Queries
>
> Use Wildcards

To gain an understanding of the above features, work through the **Driving Lessons** in this **Section**.

For each **Driving Lesson**, read the **Park and Read** instructions, without touching the keyboard, then work through the numbered steps of the **Manoeuvres** on the computer. Complete the **Revision Exercise(s)** at the end of the section to test your knowledge.

Driving Lesson 14 - Sum

Park and Read

Queries can be created in *Access*, where summary values only are displayed rather than individual records. The summary values can be displayed for the whole query, or as subtotals for certain groups of records. Common summary calculations include finding the total and average of a set of figures, the maximum and minimum value and counting the number of records. These calculations are carried out on a **Total** line within the query.

Manoeuvres

1. Open the **Premises** database which holds information on commercial properties for sale in a large city. Start a new query in **Design View**. From the **Commercial** table place the **Location** and **Price** fields on to the query grid.

2. Click on the **Totals** button, Σ, on the toolbar. A new row appears on the grid marked **Total:** with the default entry of **Group By**.

3. Click in the **Total** box for the **Price** field, then click on the down arrow to display the drop down list. Select **Sum** from this list.

Field:	Location	Price	
Table:	Commercial	Commercial	
Total:	Group By	Sum	
Sort:			
Show:	☑	☑	☐
Criteria:			
or:			

4. Run the query.

Location	SumOfPrice
Central Area	£1,237,000.00
DockLand	£525,000.00
Enterprise Centre	£574,000.00
Industrial Park	£387,000.00
Riverside Complex	£907,000.00
Valley Grove	£551,000.00

5. The records are grouped by **Location**, and the **Price** is totalled for each different location.

6. Switch back to the **Design View** and leave the query open for the next Driving Lesson.

*The **Total** row can be removed by clicking Σ again.*

Driving Lesson 15 - Count

Park and Read

The **Count** calculation is another summary calculation, which counts how many entries in a query have a value in a particular field, including duplicate values. It does not count null entries, i.e. empty fields.

Manoeuvres

1. Using the query from the previous Driving Lesson, change the **Total** box for the **Price** field to **Count**.

Field:	Location	Price	
Table:	Commercial	Commercial	
Total:	Group By	Count	
Sort:			
Show:	☑	☑	☐
Criteria:			
or:			

2. Run the query. The answer table now shows a count of how many premises (that have a price) are in each location group.

Location	CountOfPrice
Central Area	8
DockLand	6
Enterprise Centre	5
Industrial Park	5
Riverside Complex	9
Valley Grove	7

   Take care when choosing which field to use in the count. If any records on the table above did not have an entry in the price field, they would not be included in the count.

3. Switch back to the **Design View**.

4. Select **Edit | Clear Grid** to clear all columns on the grid then leave the query open for the next Driving Lesson.

Section 3 Queries ECDL/ICDL Access 2003

Driving Lesson 16 - Average Values

Park and Read

Avg is another summary calculation. It calculates the average of all values in a field. It is selected from the **Total** row in the query grid, in a similar way as **Count** and **Sum**. All summary calculations can be combined with selection criteria to obtain statistics on certain parts of the data.

Manoeuvres

1. Using the query from the previous Driving Lesson, add the field **Type of Premises**. Leave the **Total** box as **Group By**.

2. Add the field **Price** to the grid. Select the calculation **Avg** in the **Total** box.

3. Run the query. The average price for each type of premises is shown.

Type of Premises	AvgOfPrice
Conference Unit	£90,000.00
Exhibition Hall	£209,333.33
Manufacturing Unit	£90,444.44
Office Premises	£116,352.94
Store Unit	£57,285.71

4. Switch back to **Design View**. Include the **Lift** field on the query grid, leave its **Total** value as **Group by** and enter **Yes** in its criteria.

Field:	Type of Premises	Price	Lift
Table:	Commercial	Commercial	Commercial
Total:	Group By	Avg	Group By
Sort:			
Show:	☑	☑	☑
Criteria:			Yes
or:			

5. Run the query again to see the average property prices by type of premises, but this time only for properties with a lift.

Type of Premises	AvgOfPrice	Lift
Exhibition Hall	£275,000.00	☑
Manufacturing Unit	£106,000.00	☑
Office Premises	£111,083.33	☑
Store Unit	£50,000.00	☑

6. Switch back to **Design View**. Remove the **Lift** column and add a criteria of **store unit** to the **Type of Premises** column.

7. Run the query to see the average price for **Store Units** only.

8. Switch to the **Design View** and delete the **Type of Premises** column.

9. Run the query to see the average **Price** for all premises.

10. Switch to the **Design View** and clear all information from the query grid.

11. Leave the query grid on screen for the next Driving Lesson.

See the **Answers** section at the back of the guide.

Driving Lesson 17 - Maximum and Minimum Values

Park and Read

Max and **Min** are summary calculations showing the maximum and minimum values of specified fields for all selected records. A range of the highest and lowest values in a table can be displayed using the **TopValues** property.

Manoeuvres

1. Using the query from the previous Driving Lesson, place the fields **Location** and **Price** on to the query grid. Add the **Price** field again as a third column.

2. Change the **Total** box for the first **Price** column to **Max** and the second one to **Min**.

3. Run the query. The answer table should contain the maximum and minimum prices in each location.

4. Switch to **Design View** and click the **Totals** button, to remove the **Total** row from the grid. Remove one of the **Price** columns and add the **Address** field to the grid.

5. Define an **Ascending Sort** for the **Price** field.

6. Select **5** in the **Top Values** drop down box, on the **Toolbar**.

7. Run the query. Premises with the 5 lowest prices are displayed.

8. Switch to **Design View**, and change the **Price** field sort to **Descending**.

9. Select **25%** in the **Top Values** drop down box. Run the query. The top 25% of records (10 out of 40) in order of **Price** are displayed.

10. Switch to **Design View**, and select **All** in the **Top Values** drop down box.

11. Close the query without saving and close the database.

See the **Answers** section at the back of the guide..

Driving Lesson 18 - Calculated Fields: Queries

Park and Read

When a calculation is required in a query, based on the contents of one or more of the available fields, a **Calculated Field** may be used. This is a field that the user creates, to display the results of a calculation defined with an **expression**. The **expression** may involve one or more numerical fields, and involve any mathematical calculations or logical definitions. It allows, for example, two fields to be multiplied together, or for a price field to be multiplied by a percentage, or a discount applied to all values in a particular field.

The name of the new field is entered in the **Field** row of a query grid, followed by a colon, :. The expression is then entered, with field names enclosed in square brackets. Once a calculated field is defined, it can be used like any other field. It can be used for selection, for sorting, or appear in forms and reports.

The standard mathematical symbols are **Add +**, **Subtract -**, **Divide /** and **Multiply ***.

Manoeuvres

1. Open the **Pets** database.

2. Start a new query in **Design View** based on **Pet Details** and place the **Animal**, **Price** and **Number Sold** fields into the grid.

3. In the fourth column enter the following expression in the **Field:** box:

    Total Amount: [Price]*[Number Sold]

4. **Total Amount** is the new field name, **Price** and **Number Sold** are the fields and * is the mathematical operator. This is a new **Calculated Field** that will multiply the price of each animal by the number of each animal sold, and call the answer **Total Amount**.

5. Make sure the **Show** box is checked for the new field.

Field:	Animal	Price	Number Sold	Total Amount: [Price]*[Number Sold]
Table:	Pet Details	Pet Details	Pet Details	
Sort:				
Show:	☑	☑	☑	☑
Criteria:				
or:				

6. Run the query.

Driving Lesson 18 - Continued

7. The answer table will contain the total amount for each type of pet that was sold.

Animal	Price	Number Sold	Total Amount
Rabbit	£30.00	3	£90.00
Fish	£0.80	5	£4.00
Toad	£1.50	6	£9.00
Snake	£13.00	6	£78.00
Dog	£3.50	7	£24.50
Cat	£8.00	9	£72.00
			0

8. Once a calculated field has been defined it can be used in the query like any other field. Return to **Design View** and enter **>10** in the criteria for the **Total Amount** field.

9. Run the query to see only those sales records where the total sales amount is greater than **£10**.

10. Return to **Design View**. Because the calculated field has not been defined in a table, it is sometimes necessary to set the field properties manually.

11. Click in the **Total Amount** column in the query grid to select it. Click **Properties**, on the toolbar. The **Field Properties** dialog box is displayed.

12. Select **Format**, click the drop down arrow and choose **Fixed**.

13. Select **Caption** and enter the text **Sales Value £**. The **Caption** value is only displayed when the query is run, it is not shown on the query grid.

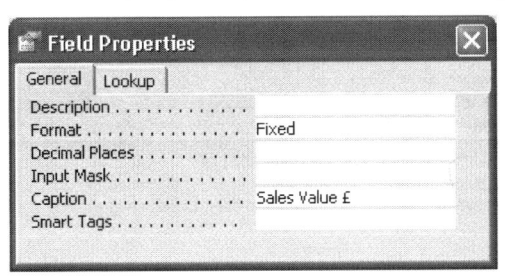

14. Close the **Field Properties** dialog box and run the query to see the changes.

15. Save the query as **Total Amount**.

16. Close the query and the database.

Driving Lesson 19 - Parameter Queries

Park and Read

If a query is being run frequently and all that is changing is the selection criteria for one or two fields, then a **Parameter Query** can be used. A **Parameter Query** displays a dialog box prompting for the criteria information. Once the information is entered, the query is performed, with the entered value being used as the selection criteria. The next time the query is run, a different value can be entered and used, without having to change the query design.

Parameters can be used together with other types of query, such as partial queries using wildcards and range queries.

A query can contain as many parameter values as required. Simply set a parameter value for each required field. Every time the query is run, a dialog box will appear for each field that contains a parameter value. The dialog boxes will appear in the order of the field names on the query grid, from left to right.

Manoeuvres

1. Open the **Premises** database. Start a new query in **Design View** based on the **Commercial** table and place the following fields on to the grid: **Location, Address, Type of Premises** and **Price**.

2. To create the parameter query, in the **Location** field enter the following text as the criteria: **[Enter Area Required]**.

   Ensure that the prompt text between square brackets is not the same as any field name. For example, [Location] would not work because there is a field with that name, but [Location?] would be OK.

3. Run the query. A dialog box appears. Notice the text entered in the criteria appears as the prompt text. The value entered in the entry box will be used as the criteria for **Location**.

4. Enter **Dockland** and click **OK**. The query is run, showing all premises in Dockland.

Driving Lesson 19 - Continued

Location	Address	Type of Premises	Price
DockLand	1 Wessington Road	Manufacturing Unit	£120,000.00
DockLand	14a The Union Buildings	Manufacturing Unit	£75,000.00
DockLand	Unit 7 Grantham House	Manufacturing Unit	£80,000.00
DockLand	17 The Port Buildings	Store Unit	£38,000.00
DockLand	Suite 15 Grosvenor Estate	Store Unit	£120,000.00
DockLand	4 Grainger Dock	Manufacturing Unit	£92,000.00

5. Switch back to **Design View**.

6. Add a criteria of **[Which Premises Type?]** to the **Type of Premises** column.

7. Run the query again. This time enter **Riverside Complex** in the **Area** prompt and click **OK**. Enter **Office Premises** in the second prompt and click **OK**.

8. Save the query as **Areas** but leave it open.

9. Parameters can be used with range selections. Return to **Design View**. Delete all existing criteria and add a new criteria to the **Price** field.

    >=[from lower value] and <=[to upper value]

10. Run the query. When the first dialog box appears, enter **100000** and click **OK**.

11. The second dialog box will appear. Enter **200000** and click **OK**. The query shows all premises with values between £100,000 and £200,000.

12. Save the query as **Values**.

13. Close the query and the database.

Driving Lesson 20 - Using Wildcards in a Query

Park and Read

The use of basic wildcard characters **?** and ***** is covered in the standard syllabus for this qualification. There are however further characters which can be used, such as **[ ]**, **!**, **-**, **#**.

Manoeuvres

1. Open the **Staff** database,

2. Create a new query in **Design View** based on the **Test List** table. Place all fields into the query grid.

3. In the criteria for **First Name**, type **T?m***. Run the query. All names starting **T?m** are listed, where **?** can be any character.

4. Switch to **Design View** and change the criteria to **T[aeo]m***.

Field:	Employee No	Surname	First Name	Position
Table:	Test List	Test List	Test List	Test List
Sort:				
Show:	✓	✓	✓	✓
Criteria:			Like "T[aeo]m*"	
or:				

*If the criteria is not formatted automatically, the query will not work and you will have to enter **Like "T[aeo]m*"** in full.*

5. Run the query. Any character from **a**, **e** or **o** is allowed as the wildcard.

6. Switch to **Design View** and change the criteria to **Like "T[!aeo]m*"**. Run the query. Any character <u>except</u> **a**, **e** or **o** is allowed as the wildcard.

7. Switch to **Design View** and change the criteria to **Like "T[a-n]m*"**. Run the query. Any character between **a** and **n** is allowed as the wildcard.

8. Switch to **Design View** and delete the criteria for **First Name**.

9. In the criteria for **Employee No**, type **Like "5##"**. Run the query. The **#** represents any number. All 3 digit numbers starting with 5 are listed.

10. Switch to **Design View** and change the criteria to **Like "##3"**. Run the query. All 3 digit numbers ending with 3 are listed.

11. Close the query <u>without</u> saving and close the **Staff** database.

Driving Lesson 21 - Revision

This is not an ECDL test. Testing may only be carried out through certified ECDL test centres. This covers the features introduced in this section. Try not to refer to the preceding Driving Lessons while completing it.

1. Open the database **Computer Shop** and create a new query in **Design View** based on the **Repairs** table.

2. Use **Group By** to find the number of engineers.

3. What are the minimum and maximum job prices?

4. What is the total price of all the jobs on the database?

5. Change the query to find the average job price grouped by engineer. Which engineer has the highest average job price?

6. Save the query as **Query21a** and close it.

7. Create a parameter query to ask for a particular engineer then show all the jobs for that engineer above an entered price. Show all fields from the **Repairs** table.

8. Use that query to find how many jobs **Keith** has that cost more than **£100**.

9. Save the query as **Query21b** and close it.

10. Close the database.

11. Open the database **Transport** and create a new query in **Design View** based on the **Buses** table. Include the fields **Fleet Number**, **Size** and **Route**.

12. Use wildcards to select only **Fleet Numbers** that have the following structure: Any 1 character followed by any 1 number followed by the number 5. What is the criteria? How many records are found?

13. Close the query without saving and close the database.

See the **Answers** section at the back of the guide.

If you experienced any difficulty completing the Revision, refer back to the Driving Lessons in this section. Then redo the Revision.

Driving Lesson 22 - Revision

This is not an ECDL test. Testing may only be carried out through certified ECDL test centres. This covers the features introduced in this section. Try not to refer to the preceding Driving Lessons while completing it.

1. Using the **Houses** database and **Property** table, create a new **Summary** query in **Design View**.

2. Use the query to display the total and average **Price** of each property grouped by **Type of Property**.

3. Which type of property has the highest average price?

4. Save the query as **Query22a** and close it.

5. Create a new query on the same table and include the fields **Location**, **Address**, **Type of Property**, **Price** and **Bedrooms**.

6. Create a new calculated field in the query, after the **Bedrooms** field. Name the new field **Rate** and define the calculation as **Price** divided by **Bedrooms**. Format the new field as **Currency**.

7. Display the query in descending order of **Rate**. Which property has the highest value for **Rate**?

8. Change the query so that it prompts for **Location** with the message "Which Location".

9. Use the query to find the property in **Rose Mount** with the highest value of **Rate**.

10. Save the query as **Price per Bedroom** and close it and the database.

See the **Answers** section at the back of the guide.

If you experienced any difficulty completing the Revision, refer back to the Driving Lessons in this section. Then redo the Revision.

Once you are confident with the features, complete the Record of Achievement Matrix referring to the section at the end of the guide. Only when competent move on to the next Section.

Section 4
Relationships

By the end of this Section you should be able to:

> Apply Primary Keys
>
> Apply and Modify Different Types of Relationship
>
> Query Related Tables
>
> Understand Joins
>
> Apply Referential Integrity
>
> Update and Delete Related Records
>
> Work with Subdatasheets

To gain an understanding of the above features, work through the **Driving Lessons** in this **Section**.

For each **Driving Lesson**, read the **Park and Read** instructions, without touching the keyboard, then work through the numbered steps of the **Manoeuvres** on the computer. Complete the **Revision Exercise(s)** at the end of the section to test your knowledge.

Driving Lesson 23 - Applying a Primary Key

Park and Read

When creating relational databases which use more than one table, it is important to be able to uniquely identify individual records in a table if they are to be referenced from another table. Records are usually identified by specifying a field in the table which contains unique data for each record, e.g. a serial number or identification number. This is then defined as the **Primary Key**.

Use of a **Primary Key** prevents duplication of records in a table and also allows sorting and querying to be performed more efficiently. It also enables the linking of tables.

Manoeuvres

1. Open the **Custom Computers** database and then the **Computers** table in **Design View**.

2. Click in the **Model** field. Click on the **Primary Key** button , on the toolbar.

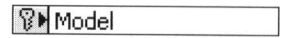

The **Primary Key** is applied to the **Model**. field. Notice in the field properties that the **Indexed** property is set to **Yes (No Duplicates)**. This means that there can be no duplicate **Model** in any two records within this table.

3. This is obviously a bad choice for the **Primary Key** field as it is likely that there will be more than one record in the table for any particular model of computer. Click in the **Serial Number** field and click on the **Primary Key** button again.

4. **Serial Number** is now designated as the **Primary Key** field. This is an ideal choice, as serial number is a unique identifier for any particular computer.

When **Serial Number** was selected as the **Primary Key**, the indicator was automatically removed from the **Model** field.

5. **Save** and close the table.

6. Open the **Repairs** table in **Design View**. A **Primary Key** is already applied to the **Job No** field.

Driving Lesson 23 - Continued

7. Notice that the **Repairs** table also contains the computer serial number field, but on this table it is not necessarily unique. There may be several repair jobs for the same computer.

8. Click the **Indexes** button, to view the **Primary Key** information.

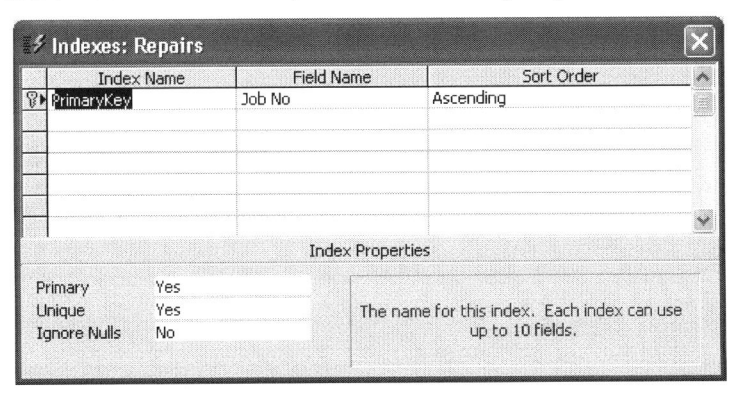

*The **Index Properties** show that a **Primary Key** field is unique and that **Ignore Nulls** is set to **No**. This means that as well as being unique, a primary key field cannot be left blank in a record.*

9. Close the **Indexes** window and the **Repairs** table.

10. Leave the **Custom Computers** database open.

Driving Lesson 24 - Applying Relationships

Park and Read

Once tables have been designed and primary keys applied, a **Relationship** may be applied between two or more tables to link them together. Once two or more tables are linked by a relationship, the data from all of the tables may be used to create a single query, form or report.

Relationships are usually applied between tables which contain a common field. Usually, the related field in the first table is the primary key field and is known as the **Primary Table**. In this way, a record in one table can link to further information on another table. The related field in the second table is known as the **Foreign Key**.

Applying relationships allows many smaller tables to be linked together to form the complete database, improving its overall efficiency. In the Driving Lesson below then, if the **Computer** and **Repairs** tables are linked using the common field serial number, there is no need to have all computer details on every repair record. A query on the **Repairs** table will use **Serial Number** to access all related data on the **Computers** table automatically.

This lesson describes the most common type of relationship, **One to Many**. Other types of relationships are introduced over the next few Driving Lessons.

Manoeuvres

1. With the **Custom Computers** database open click the **Relationships** button, on the main toolbar. The **Show Table** dialog box appears.

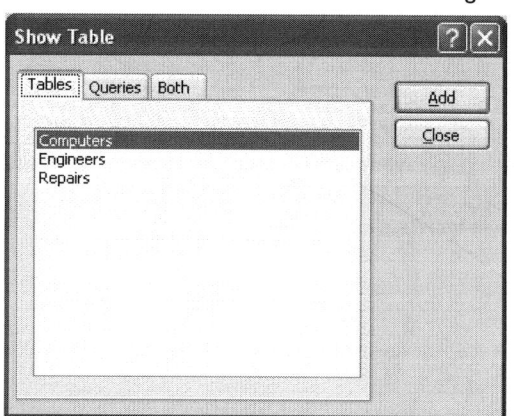

    If the **Show Table** dialog box does not appear, click on the **Show Table** button on the **Toolbar**.

Driving Lesson 24 - Continued

2. With the **Computers** table highlighted, click [Add] to place the table in the **Relationships** window.

3. Click on the **Repairs** table and again add it to the window then click [Close] to remove the **Show Table** dialog box.

4. Resize the table boxes to see all of their fields. Notice the **Primary Keys** for each table are in bold.

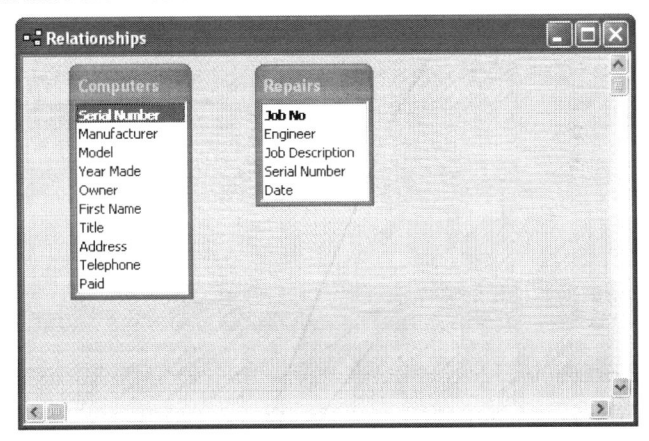

5. Highlight the **Serial Number** field in the **Computers** table.

6. Drag the **Serial Number** field, from the **Computers** table, over the **Serial Number** field (the foreign key) in the **Repairs** table. Release the mouse when in position.

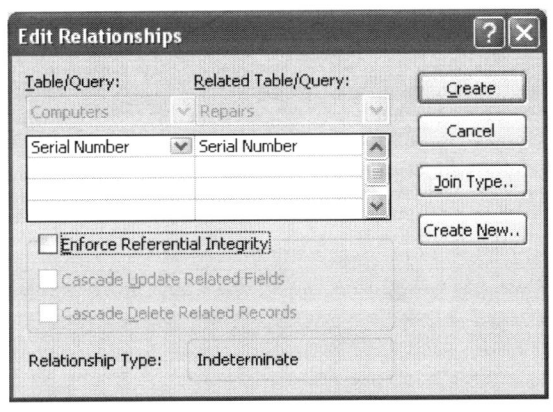

7. In the **Edit Relationships** dialog box, note the relationship type is **One-To-Many**. This is the most common type of relationship.

Driving Lesson 24 - Continued

8. Click **Create** to create the relationship.

9. Notice how the relationship between the tables is now symbolised by a line, linking the same field, **Serial Number**.

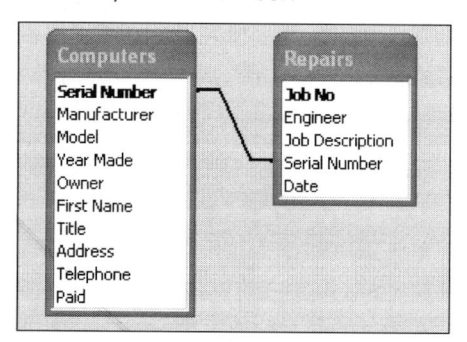

i The relationship is **One-To-Many**. This means that **one** record from **Computers** can have **many** related records in **Repairs,** i.e. one computer may have had several repairs. The fact that one of the fields in the link is a primary key and the other is not, defines the relationship as **One-To-Many**.

10. To delete the relationship, right click on the connecting line and select **Delete**. Select **Yes** to confirm the deletion.

i Any relationship can be modified by right clicking on the connecting line and selecting **Edit Relationship**.

11. Now click and drag from **Owner** in the **Computers** table to **Engineer** in the **Repairs** table.

12. This is not a valid relationship; the relationship type is shown as **Indeterminate**. Click **Cancel**.

13. Reapply the original relationship between **Serial Number** in both tables and click **Create**.

14. Close the **Relationships** window and select **Yes** when prompted to save the changes to the relationship.

15. Leave the database open for the next Driving Lesson.

Access 2003   *ECDL/ICDL*   *Section 4 Relationships*

Driving Lesson 25 - One-to-One Relationships

Park and Read

A **One-to-One** relationship is used where one record in one table is linked to only one record in another. This can be used to split a large table with many fields, or if part of a table needs to be removed for security reasons, or if the second table contains optional data which is not always required.

Manoeuvres

1. To create a **One-to-One** relationship in the **Custom Computers** database, create a table in **Design** view with two fields, **Job No** and **Charge**.

2. The **Job No** field will have a data type of **Number** and the **Charge** field will be **Currency**.

3. Make the **Job No** field the **Primary Key** and save the table as **Cost**. Close it without adding any data.

4. Open the **Relationships** window showing the existing relationship and use the **Show Table** button to display the dialog box.

5. Select **Cost** then click **Add** to add it to the **Relationships** window. Close the **Show Table** box.

6. Reposition the **Cost** table if necessary, then make the link between **Job No** in the **Repairs** table and **Job No** in the **Cost** table. Because each of these fields is a primary key, this time in the **Edit Relationships** box, the **Relationship Type** is **One-To-One**.

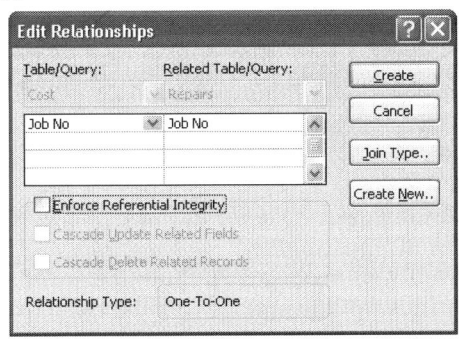

7. Click **Create**.

*As with any relationship, this can be deleted or modified by right clicking on the connecting line and selecting **Delete** or **Edit Relationship**.*

Module AM5 Database Advanced Level   47   © *CiA Training Ltd 2009*

Driving Lesson 25 - Continued

8. Close the **Relationships** window, saving at the prompt, then open the **Computers** table.

9. Click the expand subdatasheet button next to the first record.

	Serial Number	Manufacturer	Model
▶ +	C44477	Cheapo	C4
+	C4535F	Cheapo	C4

10. The related **Repairs** table is shown – notice that **Serial Number**, the related field in the second table (the foreign key), is not shown.

11. There is also now an expand button in the **Repairs** table. Click on it.

12. The **Cost** table is shown for this record.

	Serial Number	Manufacturer	Model	Year Made	Owner
▶ –	C44477	Cheapo	C4	2005	Banner
		Job No	Engineer	Job Description	Date
	▶ –	2	Stephen	Reinstall Operating System	06/04/2008
			Charge		
		▶	£0.00		
	*				
+	C4535F	Cheapo	C4	2005	Patel
+	C7689E	Cheapo	1700	2004	Bailey

13. At the moment there is no data in the **Charge** field. Add a charge of **£50** for this repair.

14. Try adding another charge for this repair. Remember there is a **One-to-One** relationship in force, so only one charge should be allowed. A warning dialog box is displayed as below.

15. Click **OK** once you have read it. To get rid of this useless information click the **Undo** button, , or press the **<Esc>** key.

16. The extra entry is deleted and the subdatasheets can be collapsed.

17. Open each subdatasheet in turn and add **Charges** for all **Repairs**.

18. Close the table and the database.

Driving Lesson 26 - Many-to-Many Relationships

Park and Read

A **Many-to-Many** relationship is used when a record in the first table can have many matching records in the second, and vice versa. For example, a single product may have many orders and a single order may be for many products. A single **Many-to-Many** relationship cannot exist. An intermediate **junction table** must be created with **One to Many** links to the two original tables. It must contain two fields: the foreign keys from both tables.

Manoeuvres

1. Open the **CiA** database. To create a **Many-to-Many** relationship between the **Orders** table and the **Products** table it is first necessary to create an intermediate, junction table.

2. Create a new table in **Design View** containing the fields **Order Ref** (**Number**) and **Product Ref** (**Text**).

3. The primary key for this new table will be defined as the combination of both fields (neither individual field will be unique on the table). Click in the area at the left of **Order Ref** to highlight the whole row.

4. Hold down <**Ctrl**> and click at the left of **Product Ref**. Both rows will be highlighted.

5. Click the **Primary Key** button, .

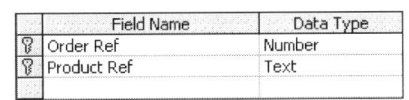

Field Name	Data Type
Order Ref	Number
Product Ref	Text

6. Save the table as **Junction** and close it.

7. This table would now have to be filled with information about which products were on which orders. Fortunately such a table already exists in the database. Open the **Order Details** table in **Datasheet View**, showing the information on each order line.

8. Switch to **Design View**.

Field Name	Data Type	
Order Ref	Number	Order reference
Product Ref	Text	Product ordered
Line Number	Number	Order Line
Amount	Number	Quantity ordered

Section 4 Relationships ECDL/ICDL Access 2003

Driving Lesson 26 - Continued

> In a working database, this table would be maintained as part of the **Order Entry** process.

9. Close the table and view the **Relationships** window. Place the **Orders**, **Order Details** and **Products** tables on to it.

10. Create a **One-to-Many** relationship between the **Orders** table and the **Order Details** table using the **Order Ref** field.

11. Create a **One-to-Many** relationship between the **Products** table and the **Order Details** table using the **Product Ref** field. The overall effect now is that there is a **Many-to-Many** relationship between the **Orders** and **Products** tables.

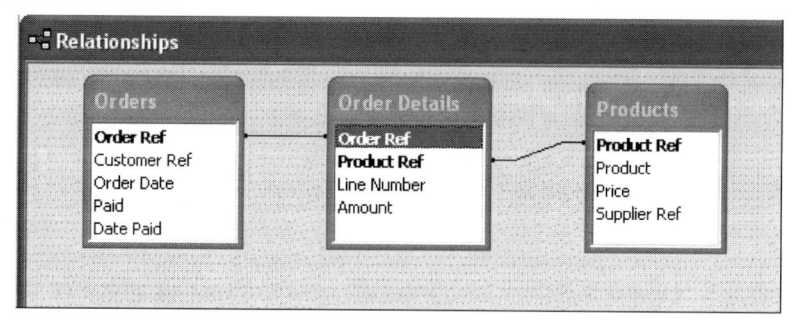

```
Relationships

  Orders              Order Details         Products
  Order Ref           Order Ref             Product Ref
  Customer Ref        Product Ref           Product
  Order Date          Line Number           Price
  Paid                Amount                Supplier Ref
  Date Paid
```

> As with any relationship, these can be deleted or modified by right clicking on the connecting line and selecting **Delete** or **Edit Relationship**.

12. Close the **Relationships** window, saving when prompted.

13. Create a query based on the three tables shown above.

14. Add **Customer Ref** and **Product** to the grid and specify an **Ascending Sort** on **Customer Ref**.

15. Run the query to see which products have been bought by each customer.

16. Switch to **Design View**, remove the **Customer** sort and specify an **Ascending Sort** on the **Product**.

17. Run the query again to see which customers have bought each product.

18. Close the query <u>without</u> saving and close the database.

Driving Lesson 27 - Applying Joins

Park and Read

Joins describe the links between tables. They affect the way queries select records when related tables are involved.

The default join type, which is applied by *Access* automatically, is an **inner join**. With this type of join, a query will only display records where there is a corresponding entry in both tables. For example, a query on linked **Computers** and **Repairs** tables would only show computers that had a repair. Any computers without a repair job, or jobs without corresponding computer records, would not be displayed. This is an important point to remember. Sometimes a linked tables query will not display all the records you expect it to because of this.

Using the above example, if you wanted to display all computers in a query, whether or not they had a match in the **Repairs** table, you would redefine the link as an **outer join** based on the **Computers** table. An alternative **outer join** based on the **Repairs** table could also be defined, which would show all repair records, even when there was no associated computer record. A **subtract join** is the opposite of an outer join; it includes only those records in one table that don't match any record in the other table.

Manoeuvres

1. Open the **Custom Computers** database and open the **Computers** table.

2. Create the following record: **B12345A**, **Bantacom**, **Pentio**, **2007**, **Smallfoot**, **Andrew**, **Mr**, **234 Cedar Drive**. Leave all other fields blank.

3. Close the table. The computer is registered but has had no repairs yet.

4. Create a new query in **Design View**. Add the **Computers** table and then the **Repairs** table to the grid. Because there is a relationship defined for these tables the link will be displayed.

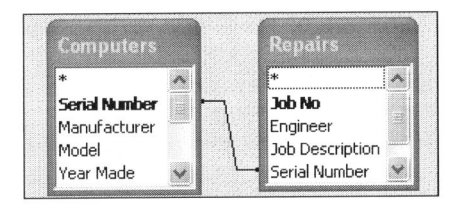

5. Double click the relationship line to display the **Join Properties** dialog box.

Section 4 Relationships   ECDL/ICDL   Access 2003

Driving Lesson 27 - Continued

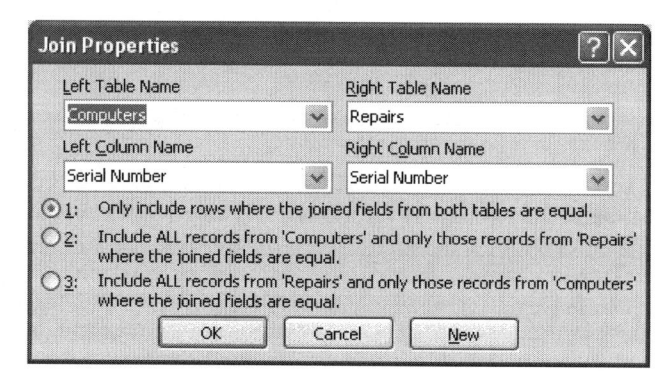

Join Properties

Left Table Name: Computers
Right Table Name: Repairs
Left Column Name: Serial Number
Right Column Name: Serial Number

- ⦿ 1: Only include rows where the joined fields from both tables are equal.
- ○ 2: Include ALL records from 'Computers' and only those records from 'Repairs' where the joined fields are equal.
- ○ 3: Include ALL records from 'Repairs' and only those records from 'Computers' where the joined fields are equal.

[OK] [Cancel] [New]

6. Notice how join type **1** is selected by default. This is an **inner join**. Click **OK** without making any changes.

7. From **Computers**, place **Serial Number** and **Model** on the grid.

8. From **Repairs**, place **Job No**, **Engineer** and **Date** on the grid.

9. Run the query. Even though the new **Bantacom Pentio** record is in the **Computers** table, it is not shown in the results because only records with repairs are displayed.

10. Switch back to **Design View** and double click the relationship line. To define the link as a **left outer join** based on the **Computers** table, select option **2**.

11. Click **OK** and run the query. The **Pentio** record is now shown, but because it has not been repaired, the last three fields are blank.

Serial Number	Model	Job No	Engineer	Date
B12345A	Pentio			
C44477	C4	2	Stephen	06/04/2008
C4535F	C4	4	David	22/04/2008

12. Save the query as **Outer join** and close it.

13. Reopen the **Outer join** query in **Design View**. Add the criteria **"Is Null"** to the **Job No** field.

14. Run the query. Only the **Pentio** record is displayed, because this is the only record without a **Job No**. This is known as a **subtract join** and displays only computers that have no repair.

[i] *The actual link is still an outer join, the Is Null criteria makes it a subtract join.*

15. Save the query as **Subtract join** and close it. Close the database.

Access 2003   *ECDL/ICDL*   *Section 4 Relationships*

Driving Lesson 28 - Self Joins

Park and Read

A **self join** describes the situation where a table needs to be linked to itself. For example, in a **Staff** table, with **Employee Number** as the primary key, there may be a field showing who each employee's manager is, using the manager's employee number. This employee number will already appear as the primary key for a record in the table (managers are also employees). To display the manager's name instead of their number in a query, a link to a copy of the **Staff** table will need to be set up, using **Manager** as the link field.

Manoeuvres

1. Open the **Staff** database and create a new query in **Design View**. At the moment, the manager that each member of staff reports to is only shown in the **Reports To** field as a staff number. A query can be created to display the manager's name, but first a **self join** must be created.

2. To create the self join, add the **Staff List** table to the query grid twice.

The table itself is not duplicated; it is just referred to by two different names.

3. The second list is given a different name, **Staff List_1**. To change this, right click on the list and select **Properties** from the shortcut menu.

4. Change the **Alias** entry to **Managers** and close the **Field List Properties** dialog box.

5. Drag the **Reports To** field from **Staff List** to the **Employee No** field in the **Managers** to create the link.

6. From **Staff List**, add **Employee No**, **Surname** and **First Name** to the grid and from **Managers**, add **Surname** to the grid again.

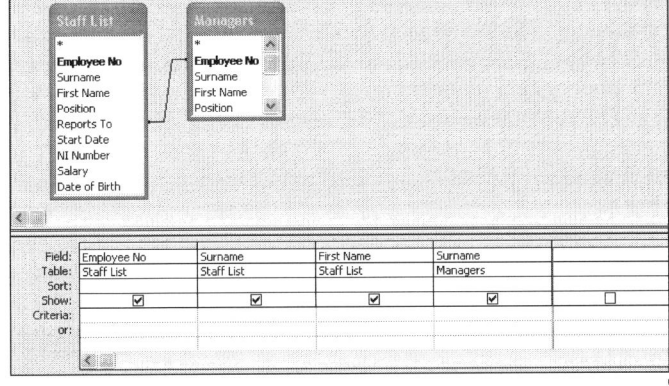

Module AM5 Database Advanced Level   53   © *CiA Training Ltd 2009*

Driving Lesson 28 - Continued

7. Click in the second **Surname** field (from **Managers**) and select an **Ascending** sort on this field.

8. To change this field title so that it displays **Manager** instead, click **Properties**, with the field still selected.

9. Change the **Caption** property to **Manager**.

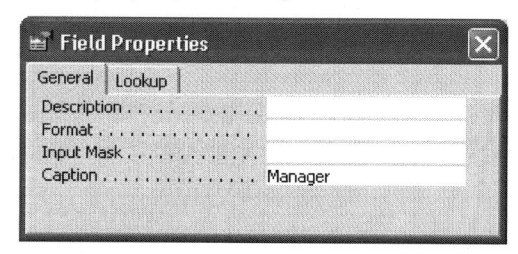

10. Close the **Field Properties** box and run the query.

Employee	Staff List.Sur	First Name	Manager
100	Nyder	Peter	Cheshunt
505	Kline	William	Cheshunt
403	Morris	Tracy	Cheshunt
301	Lee	Ciara	Cheshunt
509	Jones	Lesley	Cheshunt
704	Parr	Norma	Cheshunt
688	Chamberlain	Anthony	Cheshunt
321	Chapman	Ian	Cheshunt
500	Valdron	Brian	Myers
1000	Ripley	Ellen	Myers
101	Cheshunt	Richard	Singh
112	Myers	Anthony	Singh
536	Singh	Vikram	Singh

11. Notice how the manager's name and not their employee number appears in the **Manager** field. This is because the self join created earlier forces the query to look up the corresponding name for each employee number entered in the **Reports To** field and return that value.

The actual link in a self join is still either an inner or outer join, it is the fact that it links to a copy of the same table that makes it a self join. Like any relationship, this can be deleted or modified by right clicking on the connecting line and selecting **Delete** *or* **Edit Relationship**.

12. Save the query as **Self join** and close it.

13. Close the database.

Access 2003 ECDL/ICDL *Section 4 Relationships*

Driving Lesson 29 - Referential Integrity

Park and Read

Referential Integrity is a set of rules which can be applied to relationships, ensuring they are valid and that data is not accidentally deleted or changed. It may be applied when specific conditions are met: the matching field from the primary table is a primary key, the related fields are the same data types and both tables belong to the same database.

Enforcing referential integrity controls the updating of primary key data in the primary table and the deletion of any record from the primary table, if a related record exists elsewhere. A record cannot be added to a related table if a record does not exist in the primary table, e.g. there can be no repair record for a computer unless an associated computer record exists in the primary table.

Manoeuvres

1. Open the **Custom Computers** database and click on the **Relationships** button, to display the relationships.

2. Right click with the mouse on the relationship line between **Computers** and **Repairs** and select **Edit Relationship** from the menu.

3. In the **Edit Relationship** dialog box, check the box for **Enforce Referential Integrity** and click OK.

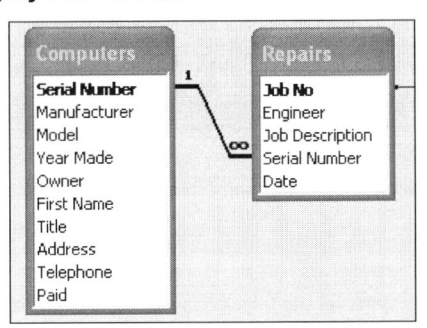

Enforcing referential integrity will change the relationship line to show the type of relationship, in this case, one to many.

4. Close the **Relationships** window.

Module AM5 Database Advanced Level

Driving Lesson 29 - Continued

5. Open the **Computers** table in **Datasheet View**.

6. Select the record **T2457** and click the **Delete Record** button, . The record cannot be deleted, as there are related records in the **Repairs** table.

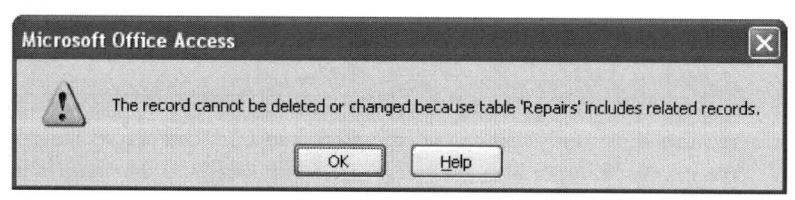

> **Microsoft Office Access**
> The record cannot be deleted or changed because table 'Repairs' includes related records.
> OK   Help

7. Click **OK**. Close the table.

8. Open the **Repairs** table in **Datasheet View**.

9. Click on the **Add New Record** button, and enter the following information:

    18, David, Renew Case, XY33, 29/06/2008

10. Press **<Enter>** after the last entry. As there is no serial number for this job in the **Computers** table, a new job record cannot be created.

> **Microsoft Office Access**
> You cannot add or change a record because a related record is required in table 'Computers'.
> OK   Help

11. Click **OK**. Delete the information just entered using **Undo**. Close the table.

12. Leave the database open for the next Driving Lesson

Driving Lesson 30 - Cascade Options

Park and Read

Enforcing referential integrity prevents the deletion or amending of records that would cause related tables to lose integrity. If **Cascade** options are set however, such deletions and amendments are allowed, but related tables will be automatically adjusted. Records in related tables will be automatically deleted or amended.

Manoeuvres

1. The **Custom Computers** database should be open from the previous Driving Lesson.

2. To allow editing or deletion of records, the relationship between the tables must be changed. Click on the **Relationships** button.

3. Right click on the linking line between **Computers** and **Repairs** and select **Edit Relationship**.

4. Edit the relationship as follows: check the boxes for **Cascade Update Related Fields** and **Cascade Delete Related Records**.

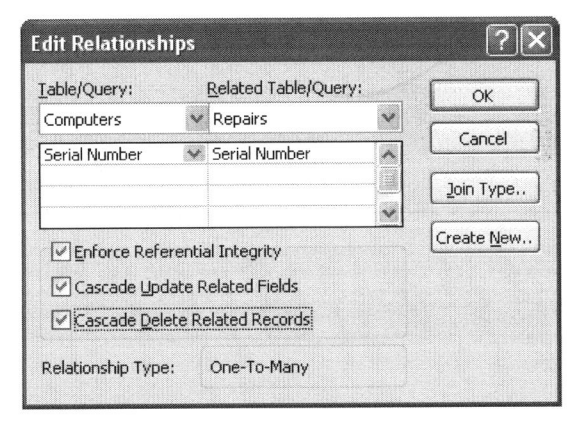

5. Click **OK**. This means that any changes made in one related table will be reflected in the others.

6. Close the **Relationships** window.

7. Open the **Computers** table in **Datasheet View** and delete the record for the **Registry Gigathon**, **R65488G**. This computer has a repair record on the **Repairs** table, record **15**.

Driving Lesson 30 - Continued

8. Deletion is now allowed but the **Cascade Delete Related Records** option means that the related records (in the **Repairs** table) will also be deleted.

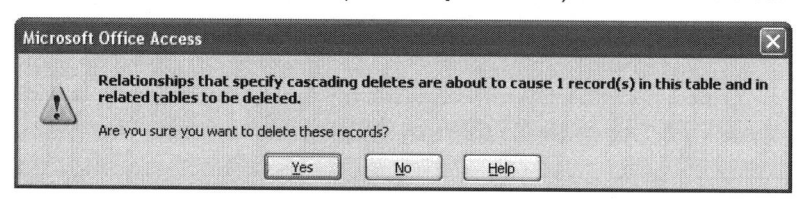

   > **Microsoft Office Access**
   > Relationships that specify cascading deletes are about to cause 1 record(s) in this table and in related tables to be deleted.
   > Are you sure you want to delete these records?
   > [Yes]   [No]   [Help]

9. Select **Yes** to continue.

*Clicking **No** would cancel the original deletion.*

10. In the **Computers** table, change the serial number **T2457** to **T5724**.

11. Close the table and open the **Repairs** table in **Datasheet View**. The **Cascade Delete Related Records** option has caused the job for the **Registry Gigathon** (job 15) to be automatically removed.

12. Look at the jobs associated with the **Triton** computer (jobs 1, 7 and 14). The **Cascade Update Related Records** option has caused the serial number for these jobs to be automatically amended.

13. Close the table and the database.

Driving Lesson 31 - Revision

This is not an ECDL test. Testing may only be carried out through certified ECDL test centres. This covers the features introduced in this section. Try not to refer to the preceding Driving Lessons while completing it.

1. Open the **Organiser** database.

2. In the **Meetings** table add a **Primary Key** to the **Meeting ID** field.

3. In the **People** table add a **Primary Key** to the **Contact ID** field.

4. Create a **One to Many** relationship between the tables using the **Contact ID** field.

5. Enforce **Referential Integrity**, with no **Cascade** options.

6. Display the **People** table. Use the subdatasheet view to see how many meetings **Ian Chapman** has recorded.

7. On the same display change the **Contact ID** for **James Tebb** to **KT**. Try to update the record. Why is the update not allowed?

8. Close all tables, redisplay the relationship between the tables and enforce **Cascade Update Fields** and **Delete Related Records**.

9. Change the **Contact ID** for **James Tebb** to **KT** again. Is the update allowed now?

10. In the **Meetings** table change the **Contact ID** field in record 5 from **GS** to **AS** and try to update the record. Why is it still not allowed?

11. Undo the last key stroke then close the table without saving any changes.

12. Close the database.

See the **Answers** section at the back of the guide.

If you experienced any difficulty completing the Revision, refer back to the Driving Lessons in this section. Then redo the Revision.

Section 4 Relationships　　　　ECDL/ICDL　　　　Access 2003

Driving Lesson 32 - Revision

This is not an ECDL test. Testing may only be carried out through certified ECDL test centres. This covers the features introduced in this section. Try not to refer to the preceding Driving Lessons while completing it.

1. Open the database **Brief Encounter**, a database for an introduction agency.

2. Open the table **Personal records** and scroll to the field **Referred by**. This uses the **BE Number** to indicate who might have referred this client.

3. Design a query that will show the name, rather than the number, of the person referring the client.

4. Show the **First Name** and **Surname** of the client and the **Surname** of the referee.

5. Change the **Caption** of this last field to **Personally referred by** and apply a **Sort** (ascending) to it.

6. Save the query as **Referrals**.

7. Use the same database to create a query showing which men have had introductions.

8. Display the **Surname** and **First Name** fields from the **Personal Records** table and the **Date of Encounter** and **Dating Number** from the **Encounters** table. Include, without displaying, any other fields that may be necessary.

9. Make sure the result will only show men.

10. Check that the join type is **inner** and run the query.

11. How many introductions are there?

12. Save the query as **Introduction**.

13. Use the same query grid to show all introductions, regardless of gender and include those that are yet to receive an introduction (change the type of join).

14. Save the query as **Dates** then close the query and the database.

[i] See the **Answers** section at the back of the guide.

If you experienced any difficulty completing the Revision, refer back to the Driving Lessons in this section. Then redo the Revision.

Once you are confident with the features, complete the Record of Achievement Matrix referring to the section at the end of the guide. Only when competent move on to the next Section.

Section 5
Forms

By the end of this Section you should be able to:

> Create Main Forms and Sub Forms
>
> Link Forms
>
> Create Forms from Multiple Tables

To gain an understanding of the above features, work through the **Driving Lessons** in this **Section**.

For each **Driving Lesson**, read the **Park and Read** instructions, without touching the keyboard, then work through the numbered steps of the **Manoeuvres** on the computer. Complete the **Revision Exercise(s)** at the end of the section to test your knowledge.

Section 5 Forms　　　　　　　　ECDL/ICDL　　　　　　　　Access 2003

Driving Lesson 33 - Main/Subform: Form Wizard

Park and Read

Just as a subdatasheet can be contained within a datasheet, a subform, containing specific, linked information, can be contained on a main form.

The easiest way to create a **Main/Subform** is to use the **Form Wizard**. A number of questions are then asked, which guide the user through the steps of creating a form with a subform.

Manoeuvres

1. Open the **Contacts** database. From the **Objects Bar** select **Forms**.

2. Double click **Create form by using wizard**. The **Form Wizard** will appear.

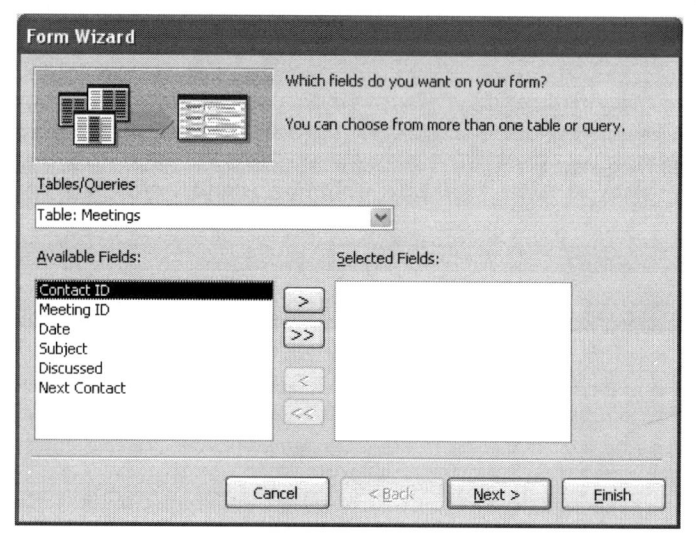

3. The wizard first needs to know which fields are to be used on both forms. From the **Tables/Queries** box, select the table **People**.

4. In the **Available Fields** box, select **Surname** then click on the `>` button to move the field to the **Selected Fields** box. Continue moving all of the fields apart from **Contact ID**, which is not needed on the form.

> Double clicking on the field names in the **Available Fields** box, will place them in the **Selected Fields** box.

© CiA Training Ltd 2009　　　　　62　　　　　Module AM5 Database Advanced Level

Driving Lesson 33 - Continued

5. Change the **Tables/Queries** box to show the table **Meetings**. This table will supply the information for the subform.

6. From the **Available Fields** box, move **Date**, **Subject**, **Discussed** and **Next Contact** to the **Selected Fields** box.

7. Click **Next**. Select to view your data **by People** and ensure **Form with subform(s)** is selected, and then click **Next**.

8. Select a **Tabular** layout then click **Next**.

9. Various predefined styles are shown. Look through the list then select **Industrial**. Click **Next**.

10. The two forms may then be given titles, if required. Leave the titles as they are and click **Finish**.

11. The new form will now appear. Maximise the window if required.

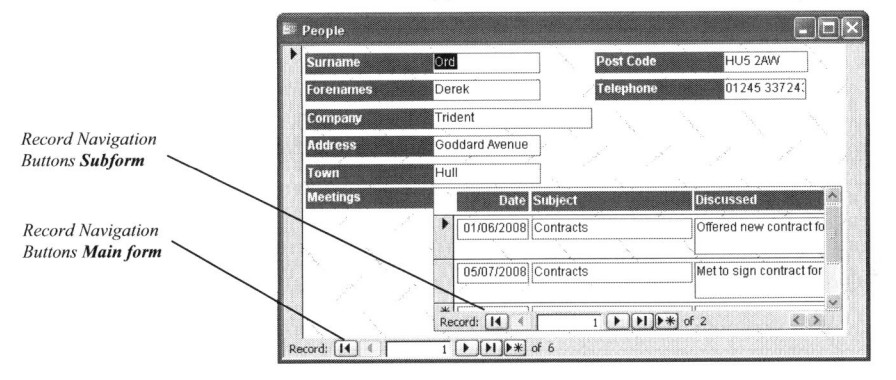

Record Navigation Buttons Subform

Record Navigation Buttons Main form

[i] As the wizard has been used to setup both the main and the subform, some of the fields may need to be resized in **Design View** so all the data can be seen on the forms. The whole subform area can be resized if required.

12. The **Main form** contains details of each person, and the contact details of that person appears in the **Subform**.

13. Use the main form record navigation buttons at the bottom of the form, to browse through the records of each person. Notice as the person changes in the main form, the meetings details change in the **Subform**.

14. Use the subform navigation buttons to move through the different meetings for each person.

15. Close the form. If prompted, to save, select **Yes** and then close the database.

Section 5 Forms　　　　　　　　ECDL/ICDL　　　　　　　　Access 2003

Driving Lesson 34 - Main/Subform: Subform Wizard

Park and Read

A **Main/Subform** can be created from two existing forms without using the **Form Wizard**. Create both forms in the normal way. Choose one as the main form, and use the **Subform/Subreport** button to add the other as a subform.

Manoeuvres

1. Open the **Computer Shop** database and click on **Forms** in the **Objects Bar**. There are two forms already created, a **Computer Data Entry** form, which will be the main form, and a **Repairs Subform,** which will become the subform.

2. Open the **Computer Data Entry** form in **Design View**. Ensure the toolbox is visible and the **Control Wizards** button, is turned **on**.

3. From the toolbox, click on the **Subform/Subreport** button, . Position the mouse under the **Address** field and click once.

4. After a few seconds the **Subform Wizard** appears.

5. Choose the **Use an existing form** option and from the list ensure **Repairs Subform** is highlighted.

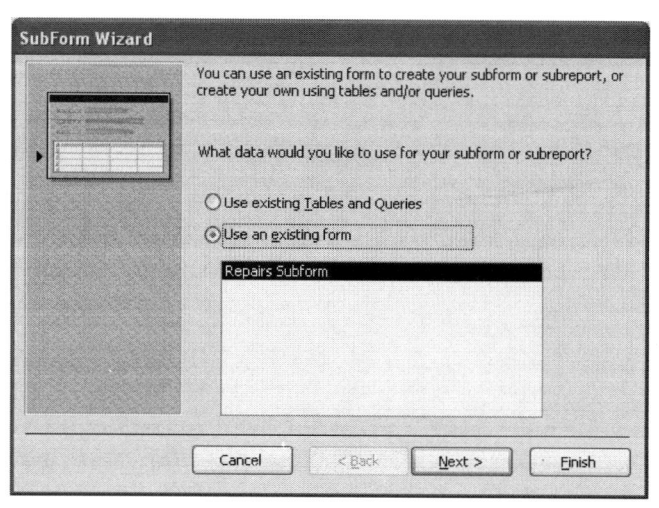

6. Click **Next**.

Driving Lesson 34 - Continued

7. Select to **Choose from a list** and **Show Repairs for each record using Serial Number**.

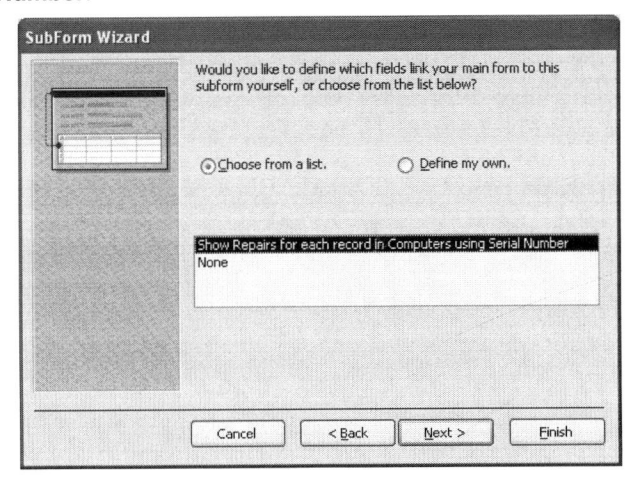

8. Click **Next**. The name for the subform is **Repairs Subform**.

9. Click **Finish** to create the subform.

10. Save the form and switch to **Form View**. Maximise the window if required.

11. Move through the computer records using the **Record Navigation** buttons at the bottom of the screen. Display record **T2457**. Using the **Subform Navigation** buttons, move through the jobs for this computer.

12. Switch to **Design View** to resize the subform if necessary, so the screen looks like the picture below. Return to **Form View** to check this out.

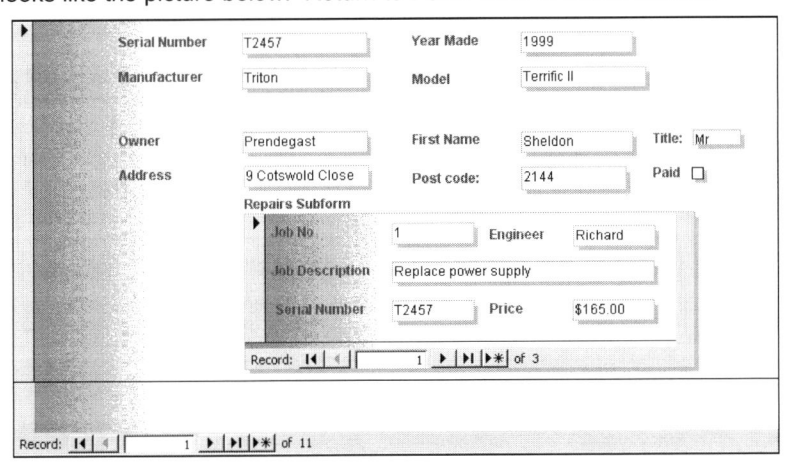

13. Save and close the form and database.

Driving Lesson 35 - Main/Subform: Manual

Park and Read

The **Main/Subform** can be created without using any wizards. With the main form in **Design View**, and the **Control Wizards** turned **off**, click on the **Subform/Subreport** button. The subform can then be manually added to the main form, and the links and design changed as necessary.

Manoeuvres

1. Open the **CiA** database. Open the **Orders** form in **Design View**. Maximise the window if necessary. If the gridlines are not displayed, they can be switched on by selecting **View | Grid**.

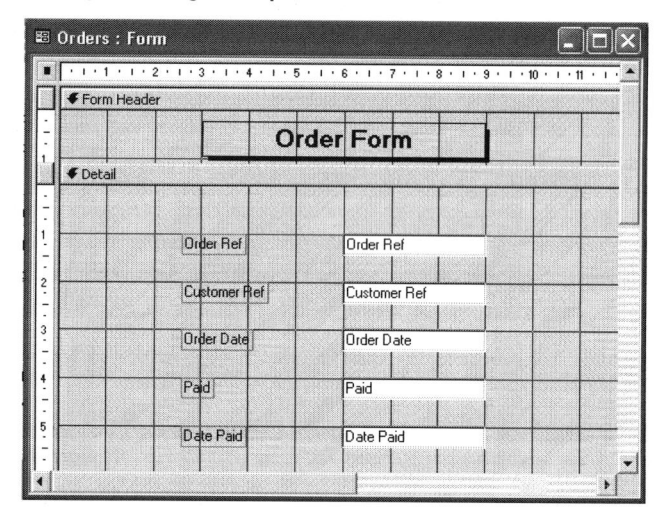

2. Ensure the toolbox is visible and the **Control Wizards** button, is turned **off**.

3. Click on the **Subform/Subreport** button, and click on the form under **Date Paid**.

4. A box appears with the word **Unbound** in it, meaning it is not linked to a particular field containing data. This is where the subform will appear, when defined. The size of this box will be changed in the following steps.

5. Click on the **Properties** button, on the **Form Design** toolbar, to view the properties for the subform. Ensure the **All** tab is selected.

Access 2003   ECDL/ICDL   *Section 5 Forms*

Driving Lesson 35 - Continued

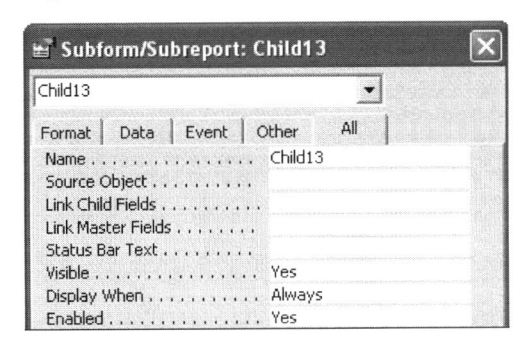

[i] *The Name **Child13** may be different on your screen but will still be correct.*

6. Click in the **Source Object** property and from the drop down arrow, choose **Order Details**. This is the table that is the **Source** of the information for the subform.

7. Ensure **Order Ref** appears in **Link Child Fields** and **Link Master Fields**.

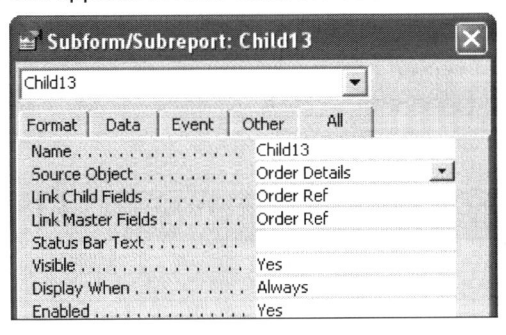

[i] *In order to make a main/subform, there must be a linking field in each table so the information in one table can pull out the correct information in the other.*

8. Close the **Properties** dialog box. Delete the **Child13** label and resize the subform so it is about **7cm** wide and **3cm** deep.

9. Save the form and switch to **Form View**. Browse through the customers. Notice that the orders list in the subform changes to show the details relevant to the viewed customer.

10. Any subform can be deleted from a form. Switch to **Design View** and click on the subform to select it.

[i] *Make sure the subform has handles around it to show it is selected.*

11. Press <**Delete**> to remove the subform.

12. Save the form and close it, then close the database.

Module AM5 Database Advanced Level   67   © *CiA Training Ltd 2009*

Section 5 Forms　　　　　　　　　ECDL/ICDL　　　　　　　　　Access 2003

Driving Lesson 36 - Linking Forms

🅿 Park and Read

Instead of creating a form with a subform within it, it is possible to create two forms which are separate, but which link together. The main form will be viewed and when a record is chosen, a button can be pressed which will open up the linked form where the relevant related data will be displayed. This approach is very useful when the main form contains a large amount of information, and the addition of a subform would clutter the screen.

Manoeuvres

1. Open the **Contacts** database. Select the **Forms** object and double click **Create form by using wizard**.

2. From the **People** table, add all of the fields apart from **Contact ID**.

3. From the **Meetings** table, add all of the fields except the two **ID** fields.

4. Click **Next**.

5. Select to view the data **by People**, and using **Linked forms**.

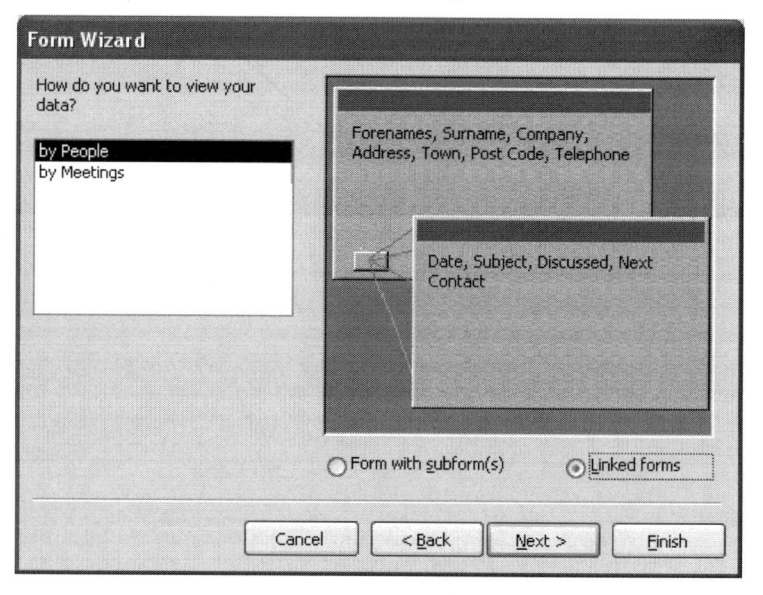

6. Click **Next**. Select a **Style** of **SandStone** and then click **Next** again.

Driving Lesson 36 - Continued

7. The title for the first form is **People Linked** and the second is **Meetings**.

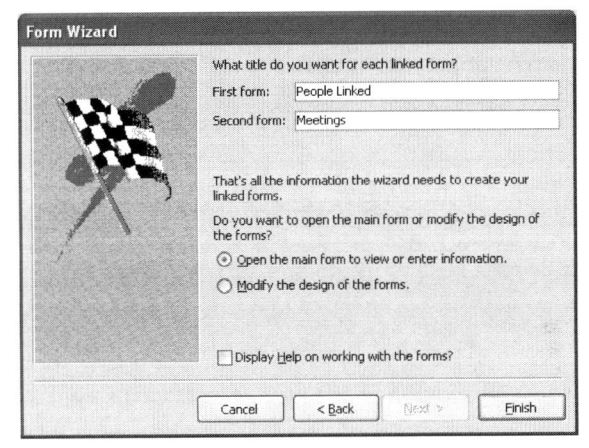

8. Click **Finish**. The form appears. Enlarge the window if necessary but do not maximise.

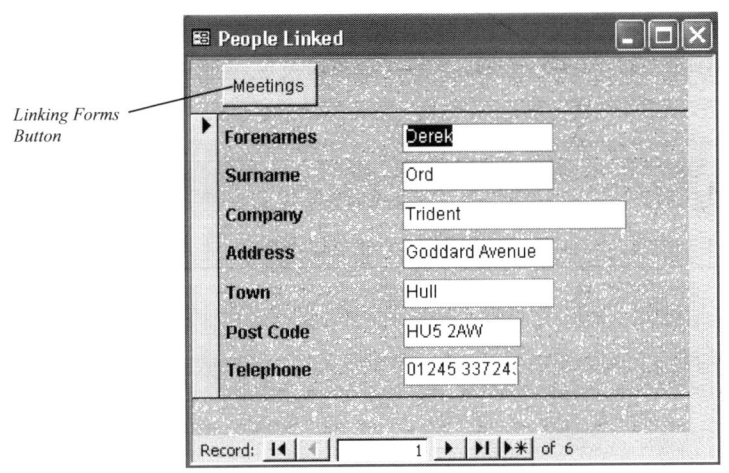

   Linking Forms Button

9. Select record number **6** and click on the **Meetings** button to open up the linked form. Enlarge the window for the second form to see all the available records if necessary but do not maximise.

10. If both forms can be seen, click on the **People Linked** form again and select another record. As the record changes, the records displayed in the linked **Meetings** form also change.

   *Alternatively, use the **Taskbar** button to switch between forms.*

11. Close both forms, saving if prompted, and then close the database.

Driving Lesson 37 - Revision

This is not an ECDL test. Testing may only be carried out through certified ECDL test centres. This covers the features introduced in this section. Try not to refer to the preceding Driving Lessons while completing it.

1. Open the **Custom Computers** database. If the **Computers** and **Repairs** tables are not already linked, do it now.

2. Create 2 new forms using **Design View**. The first form is to be the main form, based on the **Computers** table. Save it as **Sandstone Computers**. Do not use **Autoform** for this exercise as *Access 2003* may attempt to create the main form/subform automatically.

3. The second form is to become the subform, based on all the fields from the **Repairs** table. Save it as **Sandstone Repairs**.

4. Place the subform on the main form to look similar to the form below:

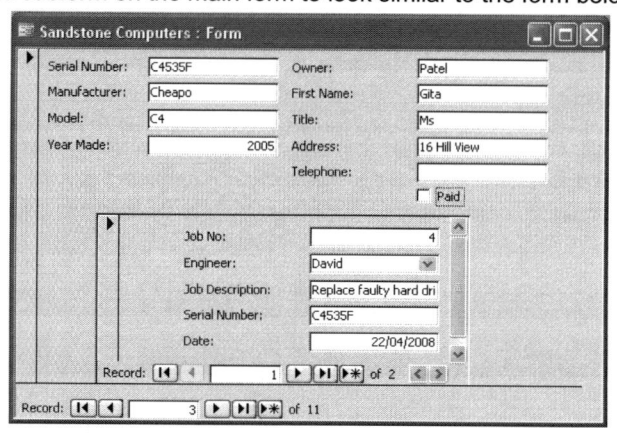

5. Save the form as **Sandstone Computers** and close it.

6. Create a query containing all the fields from both the **Computers** and **Repairs** tables but with only one **Serial Number**. Save the query as **Linked**.

7. Create an **Autoform** based on the **Linked** query. Save it as **Multitable**.

8. The navigation buttons on the **Multitable** form indicate more records than on the **Sandstone Computers** form. Why is this?

9. Close the forms and database.

See the *Answers* section at the back of the guide.

If you experienced any difficulty completing the Revision, refer back to the Driving Lessons in this section. Then redo the Revision.

Driving Lesson 38 - Revision

This is not an ECDL test. Testing may only be carried out through certified ECDL test centres. This covers the features introduced in this section. Try not to refer to the preceding Driving Lessons while completing it.

1. Open the database **Brief Encounter**.

2. Create a form with a subform for the two tables using any method (the main form is to be based on **Personal records**).

3. Save the forms as **Introduction** and **Introduction Subform**.

4. Edit the form so that all fields in the subform are displayed (it may be necessary to widen the form area).

5. Use the main form to find record 6 (Philip Baron).

6. Enter records on the subform to record meetings with Henrietta Potts and Beryl Barrington.

7. Close the form and the database.

If you experienced any difficulty completing the Revision, refer back to the Driving Lessons in this section. Then redo the Revision.

Once you are confident with the features, complete the Record of Achievement Matrix referring to the section at the end of the guide. Only when competent move on to the next Section.

Section 6
Form Controls

By the end of this Section you should be able to:

>Create the following controls:
>>Calculated Fields on Forms
>>
>>Command Buttons
>>
>>Combo Boxes
>>
>>List Boxes and Check Boxes
>>
>>Option Groups
>>
>>Add Data Fields to Headers and Footers

To gain an understanding of the above features, work through the **Driving Lessons** in this **Section**.

For each **Driving Lesson**, read the **Park and Read** instructions, without touching the keyboard, then work through the numbered steps of the **Manoeuvres** on the computer. Complete the **Revision Exercise(s)** at the end of the section to test your knowledge.

Driving Lesson 39 - Calculated Fields: Forms

Park and Read

There are different types of form controls: **bound** (gets its data from a source/field) **unbound** (not linked to a data source) and **calculated**. A calculated field uses a mathematical expression to obtain its information. These fields are calculated using other information from the database and are calculated each time they are required.

A text box is drawn on a form, and the expression entered into it. The expression may include any of the usual mathematical symbols (+ - * /) and expressions such as **Average**, **Sum**, **Max** and **Min**. When the form is viewed, the field will calculate the expression, and will recalculate as the record changes.

Manoeuvres

1. Open the **Pets** database and the **Pet Entry Form** in **Form View**. A calculated field is to be created to calculate the total value of sales for each pet, based on the price multiplied by the quantity sold.

2. Switch to **Design View**. Ensure the toolbox is visible. Click on the **Text Box** button abl, and click below the **Number Sold** field. An **unbound** control is created (not linked to data source).

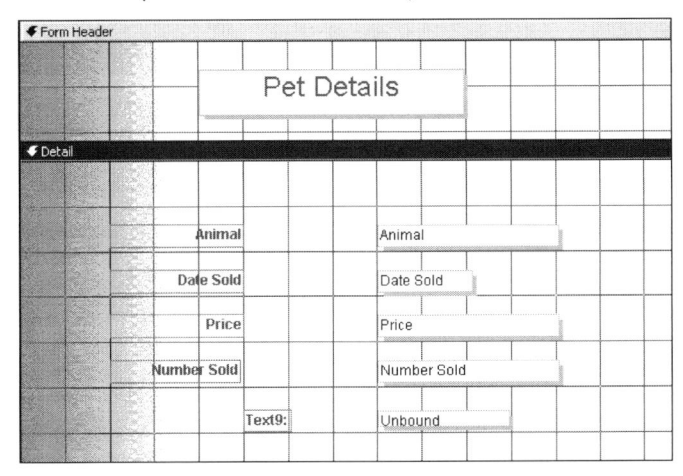

3. Click once on the new unbound box and enter the following expression:

    =[Price]*[Number Sold]

Any field names used must be entered within square brackets.

Driving Lesson 39 - Continued

4. Click on the label next to the calculated field, delete **Text9:** and enter **Total Amount**. Resize and reposition the label and field if necessary.

| Number Sold | | Number Sold |
| Total Amount | | =[Price]*[Number Sold] |

5. Display the **Properties** for the new field and select the **All** tab.
6. Type **Amount** in the **Name** box to replace **Text9**.
7. Click once in the **Format** property and from the drop down arrow, select **Currency**.
8. Add another **Text Box** below the new one. Enter the following expression:

=IIf([Amount]>50,"High value","Low Value")

[i] *This logical expression displays one of two messages, depending on the value of the calculated **Amount** field.*

9. Click on the label for the new field and delete it (be careful not to delete the field).
10. Close the properties box, and switch to **Form View**.
11. A calculation appears which is the **Price** multiplied by the **Number Sold**, with a text message below it.

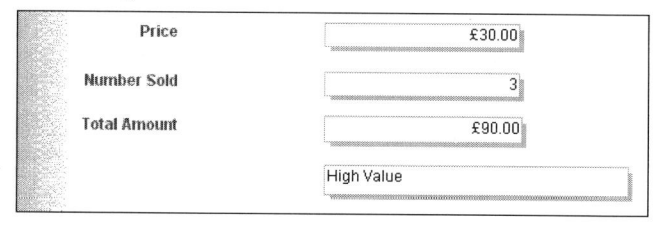

Price	£30.00
Number Sold	3
Total Amount	£90.00
	High Value

12. View the next record - the new **Total Amount** is automatically calculated.
13. Change the **Number Sold** in record **2** to **100**, then click in the **Total Amount** field. The figure is recalculated.
14. Switch to **Design View**. Change the **Total Amount** calculation to =[Price]*[Number Sold]*0.9. Change the label to **Discounted Amount**.
15. Click on the text box with the **=IIf** calculation field and press <**Delete**>.
16. Switch to **Form View** to see the effect.
17. Save and close the form and close the database.

Driving Lesson 40 - Combo Box 1: Wizard

Park and Read

A **Combo Box** is a field on a form, which will allow a value to be chosen from a drop down list or will allow a value to be entered (unless restricted by the field properties). This will speed up data entry and will stop incorrect data entry, such as spelling mistakes, etc.

There are three options to choose from, when using the wizard:

I want the combo box to look up the values in a table or query

The combo box will display the values already in a specified field in a named table. The default is to show all values, even when there are duplicates.

I will type in the values that I want

The combo box will display the values that have been typed into a list when the box was created. Values can be amended later in the field properties.

Find a record on my form based on the value I selected in my combo box

The combo box will display the values from a field in the current table. The value selected will be used to search for a record that matches the entry. It is advisable to use a field unique to each record, such as a reference number.

The following Driving Lessons cover creating a combo box using each of the options.

Manoeuvres

1. Open the **Authors** database and the **English Literature** form in **Design View**.

2. Select the **Surname** label and field and press <**Delete**> to remove both.

3. Instead of just typing an entry in **Surname**, a **Combo Box** will be used to give the option of selecting any value of surname already in the table. Ensure the toolbox is in view and the **Control Wizards** button is **on**.

4. From the toolbox, click on the **Combo Box** button. Place the mouse where the **Surname** field was and click once to create the combo box.

5. After a few seconds the **Combo Box Wizard** appears. Select the first option, **I want the combo box....**

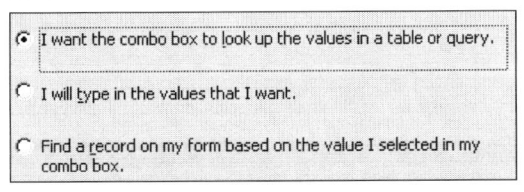

Driving Lesson 40 - Continued

6. Click **Next**.

7. The table, which contains the values to appear in the combo box, is the **Author** table. Select **Author** from the list.

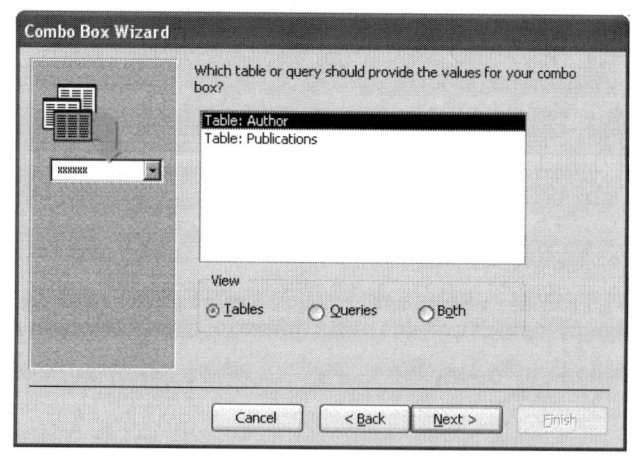

8. Click **Next**. It is the **Author Name** field that contains the values to appear in the combo box. Select **Author Name** and click **>**.

9. Click **Next** and **Next** again to ignore sorting. If necessary resize the column so all information is displayed, then click **Next**.

10. Once a value has been chosen from the combo box, it needs to be stored in the **Surname** field on the table. Select **Store that value in this field** and choose the **Surname** field.

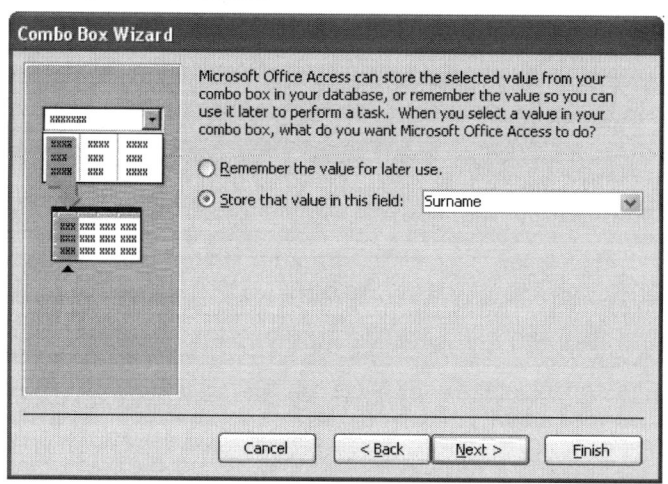

Driving Lesson 40 - Continued

11. Click **Next**. Enter **Surname** as the label for the combo box. Click **Finish**.

12. Click in the **First Name** field. Click on the **Format Painter** button, then click on the **Surname** field to copy the same format from the **First Name** field, to the **Surname** field.

13. Resize and reposition the **Surname** field as appropriate.

> The last field to be placed on the form is automatically positioned at the bottom of the tab order list, which governs the way the cursor moves around the form.

14. Because the new combo box for **Surname** was added last, it must be moved up the tab order list. To change the tab order, select **View | Tab Order** whilst still in **Design View**.

15. Click the box to the left of the **Combo** field in the **Tab Order** dialog box to select it, then click and drag it to the top of the list above the **First Name** field.

16. Click **OK** then save the form and switch to **Form View**.

17. Click on the **New Record** button at the bottom of the screen.

18. Click the drop down arrow on the **Surname** box and select **Austen** from the list.

> As this is a **Combo** field, it is possible to type in a value instead.

19. Complete the remaining fields as shown below (including the deliberate mistake).

20. Leave the form open for the next Driving Lesson.

Driving Lesson 41 - Limit to List

Park and Read

By default it is possible to type any value in a combo box, but this can be changed.

Manoeuvres

1. Ensure the **English Literature** form is open and in **Form View**.
2. Click on the **New Record** button at the bottom of the screen then click in the **Surname** field and type **Barnacle**. Press **<Enter>**. Even though this is not a value on the **Author** table it is still accepted.
3. Click the **Undo** button to reverse the entry.
4. Switch to **Design View** and display the properties for the **Surname** combo box field.
5. On the **Data** tab, change the **Limit To List** setting to **Yes**.

Row Source Type	Table/Query
Row Source	SELECT [Author].[Autho
Bound Column	1
Limit To List	Yes
Auto Expand	Yes

6. Close the **Property** box and switch to **Datasheet View**.
7. Click on the **New Record** button at the bottom of the screen then click in the **Surname** field and type **Barnacle**. Press **<Enter>**. Now the entry will not be accepted because it is not on the **Author** table.
8. Click **OK** at the message then click the **Undo** button.
9. Switch to **Design View**, select the **Surname** combo box field and press **<Delete>**. The field is removed.
10. Make sure the **Field List** is displayed and drag the **Surname** field from the list back to its original position on the form.
11. Use **Format Painter** to copy the same format from the **First Name** field to the **Surname** field.
12. Save the form and leave it open for the next exercise.

Driving Lesson 42 - Combo Box 2: Wizard

Park and Read

For a small number of values in a combo box it may be easier to look up a separate list, entered as part of the setting up process for the box itself.

Manoeuvres

1. Ensure the **English Literature** form is open and in **Design View**.

2. Delete the **Literature** field and label from the form.

3. Ensure the **Control Wizards** button is <u>on</u>. Click the **Combo Box** button, and click once below the **Title** field.

4. From the wizard select the second option, **I will type in the values that I want**. Click **Next**.

5. Specify that **1** column is required in the combo box and enter the following values, pressing **Tab** after each entry: **Prosy** (incorrectly spelt) **Drama** and **Poetry**.

6. Click **Next**. Select to **Store that value in this field** and select the **Literature** field.

7. Click **Next**. Enter **Literature** as the label and click **Finish**.

8. Resize the combo box and label as appropriate. Format it in the same way as the other fields.

9. There has been a spelling mistake in the combo box. To change values in a combo box, select the combo box and view its **Properties**. Select the **Data** tab and then select the **Row Source** property.

10. Use the ←→ keys to navigate to the **Prosy** entry, change the spelling to **Prose**.

11. From the **Limit to List** property, select **Yes**. This means that users will not be able to enter any other text; just to select from the combo box.

12. Close the properties box and save the form.

13. Switch to **Form View** and move to record number **95**. Using the new combo box, change the literature field from **Drama** to **Prose**.

14. Leave the form and database open for the next Driving Lesson.

Driving Lesson 43 - Combo Box 3: Wizard

Park and Read

A combo box can be used to find a value from the current table and use that to retrieve the appropriate record. When creating these combo boxes, it is better to include the **Primary Key** as the field in the combo box, as this is a unique field in the table and each value will successfully locate a single record.

Manoeuvres

1. With the **English Literature** form open from the previous Driving Lesson, switch to **Design View**.

2. Ensure the **Control Wizards** button is **on**. Click the **Combo Box** button, and click once in the **Form Header**.

3. From the wizard select **Find a record on my form...** Click **Next**.

4. Click on **Title** then **>**. This is the field that will be searched by the combo box, to display the desired record.

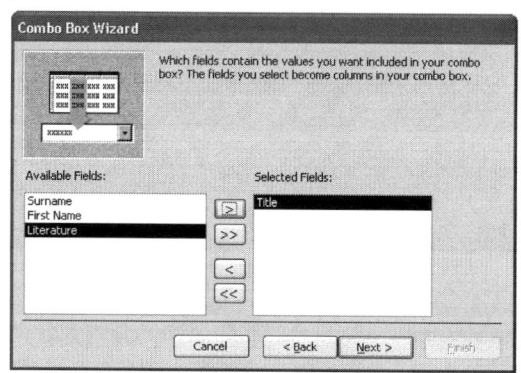

5. Click **Next**. Resize the **Title** field if necessary.

6. Click **Next** and change the **Label** text to **Title Search**.

7. Click **Finish**. Copy the format of the other fields to the new field using the **Format Painter** and reposition/resize as required. Save the form and switch to **Form View**.

8. Click on the **Combo Box** drop down arrow in the **Form Header**. A list of all the publication titles on the table appears.

9. Select any title from the list to display all the fields from the desired record. Do not select a title containing an apostrophe, the *Access* process cannot handle this without amendment to the underlying code.

10. Save the form, and leave it open for the next Driving Lesson.

Driving Lesson 44 - Combo Box: Manual

Park and Read

Combo boxes can be created without using a wizard. A combo box can be placed on to the form with the **Control Wizards** feature turned **off**. The properties of the combo box will be set up separately.

Manoeuvres

1. Open the **Premises** database and open the **New Premises** form.

2. Change to **Design View** and ensure that **Control Wizards** is turned **off**.

3. Delete the **Location** field from the form.

4. Use the **Combo Box** button, to create a combo box where the field was previously.

5. With the combo box selected click the **Properties** button. Select the **All** tab to view all the properties.

6. Click in the **Row Source** property and click on the **Build** button. The **Show Table** dialog box and **Query Builder** window appear.

7. Select the **Commercial** table. Click **Add** then **Close**. Add the **Location** field to the query grid.

8. Close the **Query Builder** selecting **Yes** to save the changes. An expression appears in the **Row Source** property.

```
Input Mask . . . . . . . . . . . .
Row Source Type . . . . . . . .  Table/Query
Row Source . . . . . . . . . . . .  SELECT Commercial.Location FROM Commercial;
Bound Column . . . . . . . . . .  1
```

9. Switch to **Form View** and click the drop down arrow in the **Location** field. All the current locations are listed but there is a lot of duplication.

10. Switch back to **Design View** and display the **Properties** box for the **Location** field.

11. Click in the **Row Source** property and click on the **Build** button. The **Query Builder** window appears.

Driving Lesson 44 - Continued

12. Right click anywhere in the **Query Builder** window (except the **Commercial** field list box) and select **Properties** from the menu.

13. Set the **Unique Values** property to **Yes**. This selects only **Distinct** values, i.e. it will stop any duplicate values being shown in the combo box.

14. Close the **Query Builder** dialog box selecting **Yes** to save the changes. The expression in the **Row Source** property has changed.

    Row Source . . . . SELECT DISTINCT Commercial.Location FROM Commercial;

*Increase the size of the dialog box if all the **Row Source** cannot be seen.*

15. Select the **Control Source** property and from the drop down list choose **Location**. This stores information from the **Combo Box** into the **Location** field. The field therefore is now defined as a **Bound Control**.

16. Close the **Properties** box. Change the combo box label to **Area** and if necessary use **Format Painter** to make sure the field matches others on the form.

17. Move the new combo box field to second in the **Tab Order** list (below **Property Ref**) by selecting **View | Tab Order**. Save the form and switch to **Form View**.

18. Create a new record (Ref **P022**) and use the combo box to select **Dockland**. Complete the rest of the fields on the form. Close the form but not the database.

Driving Lesson 45 - List Boxes

Park and Read

List Boxes are similar to combo boxes except the options are permanently viewed in a list format, and no manual entry is allowed. The amount of values which appear in the box depends on the size of the list box you create. If the list box is too small, scroll bars will appear to the side of the list box, to allow you to scroll through the values.

Manoeuvres

1. With the **Premises** database open from the previous Driving Lesson, open the **New Premises** form in **Design View**.

2. Ensure the toolbox is visible and the **Control Wizards** button is **on**. Delete the **Glazing** field in the **Detail** section.

3. Make a **3cm** space available at the top of the second column by moving any existing fields down the form.

4. From the toolbox, select the **List Box** button  and click once at the top right of the form detail area. After a few seconds the **List Box Wizard** appears.

5. Notice that the options for a list box are exactly the same as for a combo box. Select **I will type in the values…** and click **Next**.

6. Type in **None**, **Standard**, **Tinted** and **Double**, using <Tab> to move to a new line after each entry.

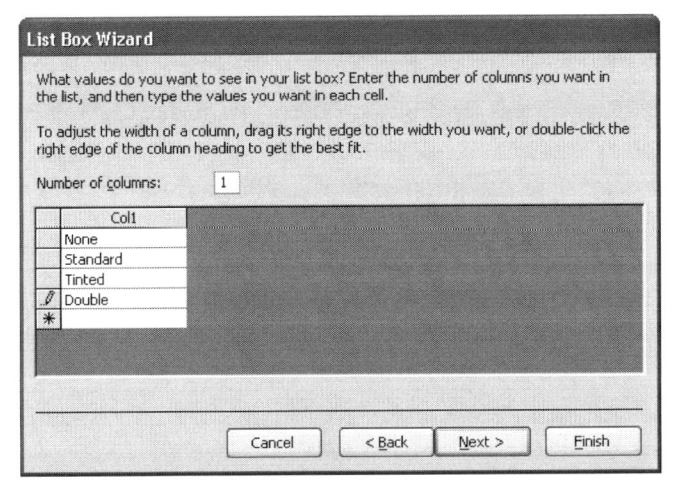

Driving Lesson 45 - Continued

7. Click **Next**, choose **Store that value in this field** and select the **Glazing** field. Click **Next**.

8. Enter the label as **Glazing** and click **Finish**.

9. Use **Format Painter** to standardise the appearance of the new field if necessary, then reposition/resize the field until the form has a similar layout to the diagram below.

10. Save the form and switch to **Form View**. Make sure record **M001** is displayed.

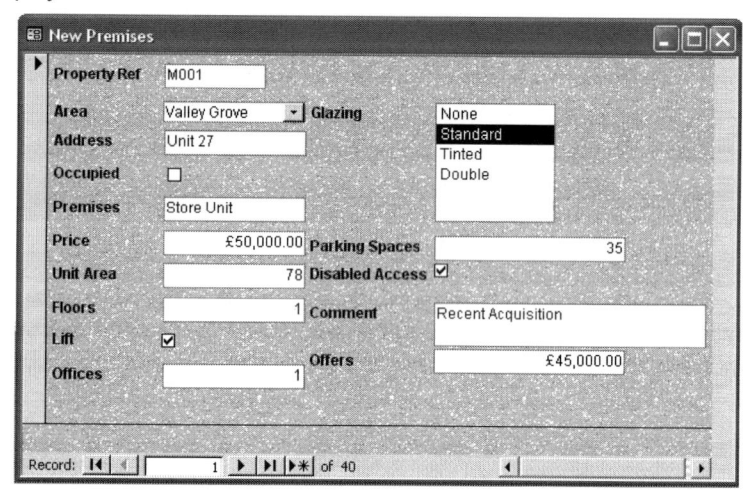

11. The list box shows all the values that can be entered into the **Glazing** field. The value for the current record is the one that is highlighted.

12. To change the value for the record on the screen, click on **Double**.

13. Start a new record and notice that nothing is selected in **Glazing** by default.

14. Switch to **Design View** and view the properties for the list box. On the **All** tab, enter **Standard** in the **Default Value** property.

15. Switch to **Form View** and start a new record. Notice now that **Standard** is selected in the **Glazing** field.

16. Switch to **Design View** and decrease the depth of the **Glazing** list box to about half of its current size.

17. Return to **Form View**. The list box should now require scroll bars to enable all the available values to be viewed.

18. Leave the form and database open for the next Driving Lesson.

Access 2003   ECDL/ICDL   *Section 6 Form Controls*

Driving Lesson 46 - Check Boxes

Park and Read

Check box controls can be added to forms when a **Yes/No** type of answer is required, i.e. check the box for **Yes**.

Manoeuvres

1. Display the **New Premises** form from the previous Driving Lesson in **Design View**. The fields **Occupied**, **Lift** and **Disabled Access** are defined in the table as **Yes/No** fields and therefore check boxes have been assigned to them by default when they were included in the form.

2. Close the form and open the **Commercial** table in **Design View**.

3. View the field properties for the **Occupied** field and click the **Lookup** tab.

General	Lookup	
Display Control	Check Box	

4. The **Display Control** property defines how the field will be displayed and by default it is set to **Check Box** for a **Yes/No** field.

*The alternative display options are **Text Box** or **Combo Box**.*

5. Close the **Commercial** table and open the **New Premises** form in **Design View**. Make sure the **Control Wizards** button is **on** and the **Field List** is displayed.

6. Drag the **Public Address** field onto the form below the **Offers** field. It appears as a check box.

7. With the field on the form still selected, press <**Delete**>. The check box is removed.

8. Check boxes can be added manually. Click the **Check Box** button, from the **Toolbox** and click underneath **Offers**.

9. View the properties for the check box (not the label). Select the **All** tab and change the **Name** to **Public Address**.

10. Click in **Control Source** and click the drop down arrow on the right.

11. Scroll down the list and select the **Public Address** field as the source to be attached to this check box. Close the **Properties** box.

12. Change the label to **Public Address**, move it to the left of the check box, then save the form and switch to **Form View**.

13. Close the form and the database.

Module AM5 Database Advanced Level   © *CiA Training Ltd 2009*

Section 6 Form Controls　　　　ECDL/ICDL　　　　Access 2003

Driving Lesson 47 - Option Groups

Park and Read

Option Groups allow a selection to be made from a number of option buttons. Only one option can be chosen from any group.

Manoeuvres

1. Open the **Authors** database and the **English Literature** form in **Design View**.

2. Ensure the **Toolbox** is visible and the **Control Wizards** button is **on**.

3. Delete the **Literature** combo box.

4. Click the **Option Group** button, from the toolbox. Click on the form where the field has been deleted. The **Option Group Wizard** appears.

5. Enter the **Label Names** as **Drama**. Press **<Tab>**, then enter **Prose** and finally **Poetry**.

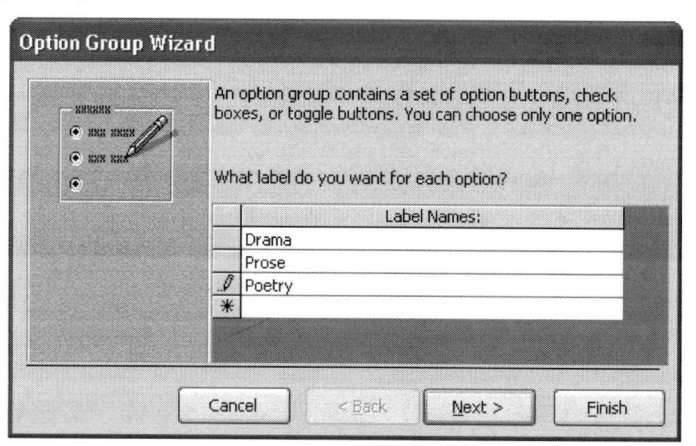

6. Click **Next**.

7. There is no default choice so select **No I don't want a default**. Click **Next**.

8. This dialog box specifies the values that are to be assigned to the choices. Using an option group means that instead of storing actual text on the table, all that is stored is a number representing the choice, e.g. the field in the table will contain **1** instead of **Drama**, **2** instead of **Prose** and **3** instead of **Poetry**. Click **Next** to accept these defaults.

© CiA Training Ltd 2009　　　　86　　　　Module AM5 Database Advanced Level

Driving Lesson 47 - Continued

9. Specify to **Store this value in this field** and select the **Literature** field. Click **Next**.

10. This dialog box specifies the type of buttons and style that are to be used. Select the different buttons and styles to see the effect.

11. Choose **Option buttons** and the **Style** as **Sunken**.

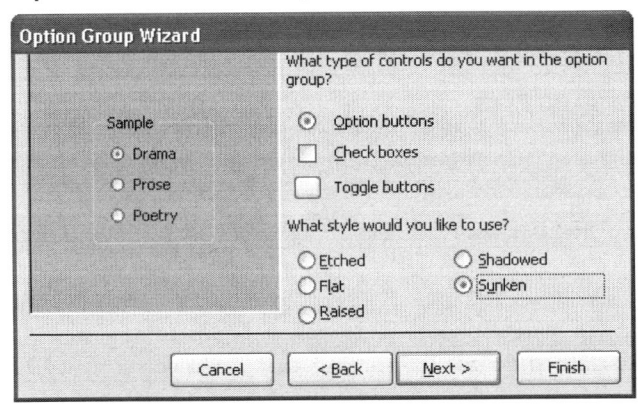

12. Click **Next**. Enter **Classification** as the caption and click **Finish**.

13. Use **Format Painter** to standardize the appearance of the option group captions, then resize/reposition if necessary.

14. Save the form and switch to **Form View**.

15. View the first record. Click **Poetry** to set this option for the first record. Set records **2** and **3** as **Prose**.

16. Close the form and open the **Publications** table to see how this has affected values in the **Literature** column. Note that only data processed through the form is affected, other records are unchanged.

17. Close the table and open the **English Literature** form in **Design View**.

18. Click the edge of the **Option Group** to select it. Display the properties.

> Make sure the whole group is selected, not just an individual button or label. The **Name** as shown in the **Properties** box should be **Frame28** or similar.

19. Select the **Format** tab and change the **Special Effect** to **Shadowed**.

> With the option group selected, pressing **<Delete>** will remove the whole group and contents.

20. Switch to **Form View** to see the effect then save the form, close it, and close the database.

Driving Lesson 48 - Form Headers and Footers

Park and Read

Forms can have Header and Footer areas defined which appear at the beginning and end of every form. Page Headers and Footers are only seen when the forms are printed and appear at the top and bottom of every printed page. Data fields can be added to header and footer areas. These can include fields from the field list or the date and time. Automatic page numbering can be added to Page Headers or Footers.

Manoeuvres

1. Open the **Premises** database and open the **New Premises** form in **Design View**. Select **View | Form Header/Footer**.

2. Drag the **Address** field from the field list to the centre of the **Form Header** area. Change the label text to **Property**.

3. To insert the date in the header, click in the **Form Header** area. Select **Insert | Date and Time**.

4. In the **Date and Time** dialog box, remove the check from **Include Time**.

5. Leave all other settings as they are and click **OK**. The date is inserted as a field.

6. Switch to **Form View** to see the actual date, then return to **Design View**.

7. To add page numbers, select **Insert | Page Numbers** and choose the **Page N of M** format, the position as **Bottom of Page [Footer]** and **Center Alignment**.

8. Normally numbers are shown on all pages, but to stop numbering on the first page remove the check as in the diagram opposite.

9. Click **OK**. Notice that **Page Header** and **Footer** areas have now been added to the design.

10. Select **File | Print Preview** to see the form as it would be printed. Page numbers will only be visible from page 2 onwards.

11. Close form, saving when prompted, then close the database.

Driving Lesson 49 - Command Button: Wizard

Park and Read

A **Command Button** is a control on a form which can be clicked to perform an action, such as closing forms, opening reports, printing, etc.

An easy way to define a command button is to use the **Command Button Wizard**, which takes the user through the steps of creating a button.

Manoeuvres

1. Open the **Pets** database and open the **Pet Entry Form** in **Design View**.

2. Ensure the toolbox is visible and the **Control Wizards** button,ptuce, is turned **on**. Click on the **Command Button**, and click once on the right side of the **Form Header** to create a button.

3. In the **Command Button Wizard** dialog box, click on the different **Categories** and view what **Actions** can be applied to a command button.

4. Select **Record Operations** from **Categories** and **Add New Record** from **Actions**.

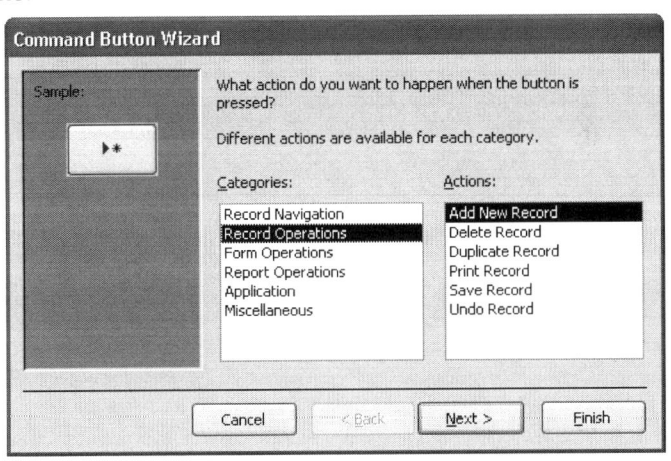

5. Click **Next**. This screen defines how the button will appear on the form. Select the **Text**, option, press **<Tab>** and enter the text: **New Record**.

6. Click **Next**. The button now needs to be given a name, so that it can be referred to later. Call the button **Add New** then click **Finish**.

7. Switch to **Form View**. Click the **New Record** button to automatically display a new, blank record.

8. Save the form and close the database.

Driving Lesson 50 - Revision

This is not an ECDL test. Testing may only be carried out through certified ECDL test centres. This covers the features introduced in this section. Try not to refer to the preceding Driving Lessons while completing it.

1. Open the **Custom Computers** database.
2. Create a columnar autoform based on the **Repairs** table.
3. Remove the **Serial Number** field and label from the form.
4. Replace it with a **Combo Box** field that will look up values from the **Serial Number** field in the **Computers** table. Store the selected value in the **Serial Number** field in the **Repairs** table. Use **Serial No** as the label for the combo box field.
5. Check that the new field drops down a list of all available serial numbers.
6. Create a command button in the footer of the new form. Define the button so that clicking on it will print out a copy of the **Repairs** table. This option is in the **Miscellaneous** category.
7. Format the button as desired.
8. Switch to **Form View** and test the use of the command button.
9. Save the new form as **View Repairs**.
10. Close the form, then close the database.

If you experienced any difficulty completing the Revision, refer back to the Driving Lessons in this section. Then redo the Revision.

Driving Lesson 51 - Revision

This is not an ECDL test. Testing may only be carried out through certified ECDL test centres. This covers the features introduced in this section. Try not to refer to the preceding Driving Lessons while completing it.

1. Open the **Houses** database and open the **Data Entry** form in **Design View**.

2. Move the **Address** field and the **Location** field into the **Form Header** area. Delete the labels for these two fields.

3. In the space left in the **Detail Area**, insert a **List Box** which displays a list of typed values: **House**, **Apartment**, **Town House**. Store the selected value in the **Type of Property** field and name the field **Type**.

4. Adjust the size of the **List Box** to fit the space.

5. Delete the **Bedrooms** field and insert an **Option Group** on the right of the form.

6. The **Option Labels** are **One**, **Two**, **Three**, **Four** and **More**, with no default.

7. Accept the default values of **1**, **2** and **3**, etc. and store the value in the **Bedrooms** field.

8. Select any style desired and set a caption of **Bedrooms**.

9. Save the form and switch to **Form View**.

10. Move to record **5** and change the number of bedrooms to **Four**.

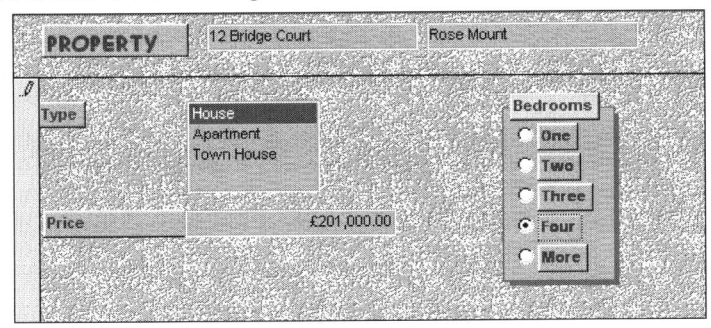

11. Close the form and close the database.

If you experienced any difficulty completing the Revision, refer back to the Driving Lessons in this section. Then redo the Revision.

Once you are confident with the features, complete the Record of Achievement Matrix referring to the section at the end of the guide. Only when competent move on to the next Section.

Section 7
Reports

By the end of this Section you should be able to:

> Create Grouped Reports
>
> Create Subreports
>
> Insert Page Breaks
>
> Create Calculated Fields in Reports
>
> Calculate Percentages
>
> Insert Data Fields in Headers and Footers
>
> Print Reports

To gain an understanding of the above features, work through the **Driving Lessons** in this **Section**.

For each **Driving Lesson**, read the **Park and Read** instructions, without touching the keyboard, then work through the numbered steps of the **Manoeuvres** on the computer. Complete the **Revision Exercise(s)** at the end of the section to test your knowledge.

Driving Lesson 52 - Grouped Report: Wizard

Park and Read

Information within a report can be **grouped**, so that records which contain the same information in a particular field, can appear grouped together on the report. Sorts can also be applied within the groups.

Manoeuvres

1. Open the **Premises** database.

2. Click **Reports**, then double click **Create report by using wizard**.

3. Ensure the **Commercial** table is selected in the **Tables/Queries** box. Select **Location** from **Available Fields** and click **>** to move it into **Selected Fields**. Similarly select **Address**, **Type of Premises** and **Price**.

4. Click **Next**. The report is to be grouped by **Location**. Select the **Location** field and click on **>** to create the grouping.

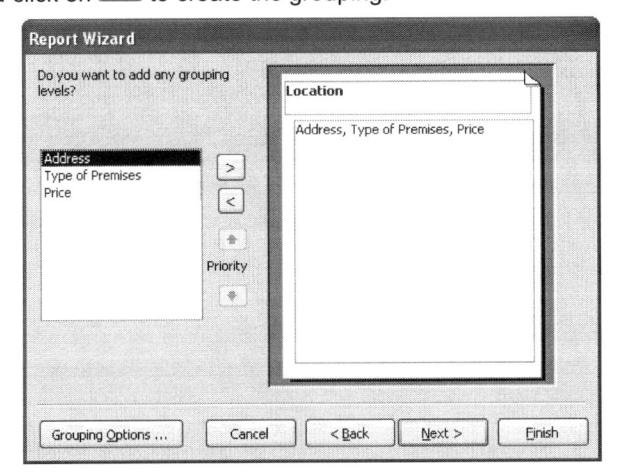

5. Click **Next**. Sort in **Ascending** order of **Price**.

Driving Lesson 52 - Continued

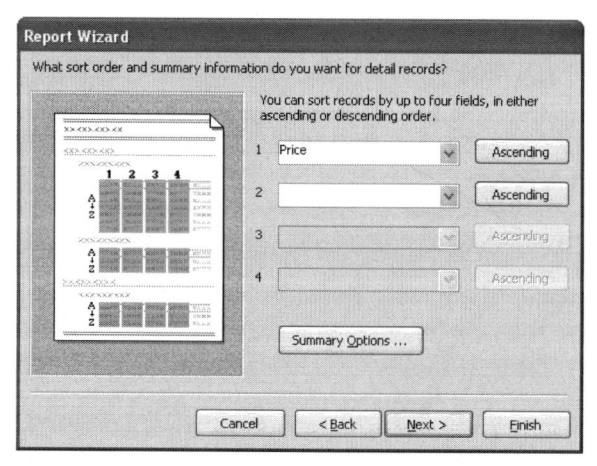

6. Click **Summary Options** to see a matrix of numeric fields and summary types. Select the option to calculate **Sum** of **Price**. Click **OK**.

7. Click **Next**. Choose the **Stepped Layout** and a page orientation of **Landscape**. Click **Next**.

8. Choose the **Corporate** style and click **Next**.

9. Name the report **Grouped Location** and click **Finish** to view the report.

10. The properties are all grouped by **Location** and appear in **Price** order within that location. The **Sum** of prices appears automatically in a special summary area for each **Location**.

11. To make the **Price Sum** field a running total rather than a separate total for each group, switch to **Design View**.

12. Right click the **=Sum([Price])** field in the **Location Footer** and select **Properties** from the shortcut menu.

13. Select the **Data** tab, click the **Running Sum** property and click the drop down arrow.

14. Select the **Over Group** option and preview the report. The **Price Sum** total field is now cumulative for each group, so that the total value for the last group is the same as the report **Grand Total**.

15. Switch to **Design View** and change the **Running Sum** property for the **Location Footer** total to **Over All**.

16. Preview the report. The group totals are now cumulative over the whole report, but because there is only one level of grouping the results are the same as before.

17. Close the report, saving any changes, then close the database.

Driving Lesson 53 - Grouped Report: Manual

🅿 Park and Read

Grouped reports can also be created without using a wizard.

🖐 Manoeuvres

1. Open the **Contacts** database.

2. Create a query which contains all the fields from both tables except any of the **ID** fields. Save the query as **Appointments** and close it.

3. From the **Database** window click on **Reports** then click on **New**.

4. Choose to create the report in **Design View** using the **Appointments** query.

5. Adjust the page width to be **15cm**.

6. From the toolbar click on the **Sorting and Grouping** button, to view the **Sorting and Grouping** dialog box.

7. Click in **Field/Expression** and from the drop down arrow, select **Subject**. Set the **Sort Order** to **Descending**.

8. At the bottom of the **Sorting and Grouping** dialog box, the **Group Properties** appear. Set **Group Header** and **Group Footer** to **Yes**.

9. Set **Keep Together** to **Whole Group**.

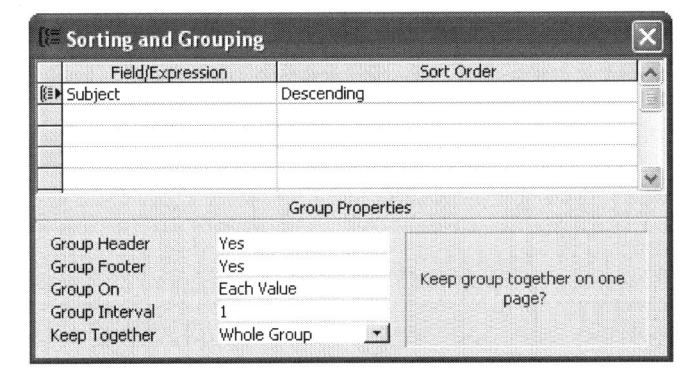

Field/Expression	Sort Order
Subject	Descending

Group Properties

Group Header	Yes
Group Footer	Yes
Group On	Each Value
Group Interval	1
Keep Together	Whole Group

Keep group together on one page?

10. Close the **Sorting and Grouping** dialog box.

Driving Lesson 53 - Continued

11. Two new sections appear in the report, **Subject Header** and **Subject Footer**.

12. Place the **Subject** field in the **Subject Header**. Remove the label and increase the **Font Size** of the **Subject** field to **12** and make it **Bold**. Apply a **Special Effect** of **Shadowed** and resize the field if necessary.

13. Within the **Subject Header** draw a line under the **Subject** field using the **Line** tool, .

14. Place the following fields into the **Detail** section, rearranging and resizing as necessary:

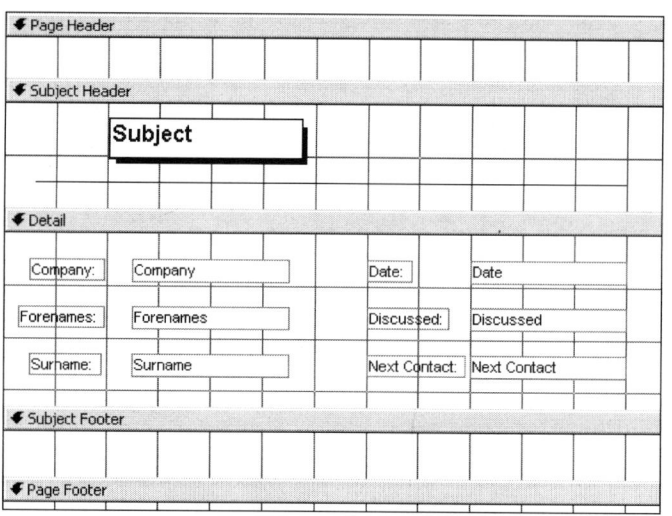

15. Save the report as **Grouped Subjects**. Click on the **Print Preview** button to preview the report. Note the number of pages.

16. Look at the first page. All the records for each subject are grouped together. Return to **Design View**.

17. Double click on the **Subject Header** section selector to show the properties for this section. Select the **All** tab and set the **Force New Page** property to **Before Section** so that each group will appear on a new page.

*Page breaks can be forced in any section of a report by double clicking the appropriate section selector and setting the required **Force New Page** property.*

18. Close the properties box and preview the report again. Notice how each group is on a new page and the number of pages has increased.

19. Close **Print Preview**. Close the report and database, saving any changes.

Driving Lesson 54 - Subreports

Park and Read

Just as a subform can be contained within a main form, a subreport containing specific, linked information, can be contained on a main report.

The easiest way to create a main/subreport is to use the **SubReport Wizard**. A number of questions are then asked to guide you through the steps.

Manoeuvres

1. Open the **Transport** database and create a new **Columnar AutoReport** from the **Buses** table.

2. Save the report as **Bus Report** and view it in **Design View**.

3. Increase the height of the **Detail** area.

4. With the **Control Wizard** on, click **Subform/Subreport**, and click in the **Detail** area beneath the existing fields.

5. From the **SubReport Wizard**, select to **Use an existing report or form** and select the **Servicing History** report.

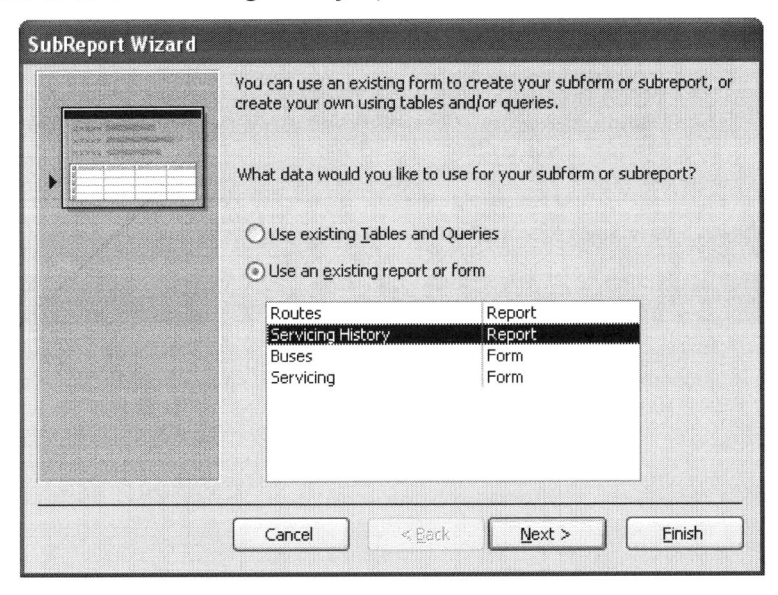

6. Click **Next**.

Section 7 Reports   ECDL/ICDL   Access 2003

Driving Lesson 54 - Continued

7. Select to **Choose from a list** and select to **Show Servicing Records for each record in Buses using Fleet Number**.

8. Click **Next** and accept the subreport name **Servicing History**.

9. Click **Finish**, then save and view the report.

10. Click **Setup** and on the **Page** tab, change the orientation to **Landscape**.

Buses

Fleet Number	B47
Capacity	55
Size	Single
Route	22
Journeys	2
First Name	Pat
Surname	Phillips

Servicing History

	Date	Repair	Logged
	14-Aug-08	Gear box	✓

[i] *The column headings in the **Servicing History** report were included in the report header area so that they would be displayed when the report was used as a subreport.*

11. View the report using the navigation buttons.

12. Switch to **Design View** and select the subreport. Check that **Servicing History** is displayed in the **Properties** dialog box.

13. Press **<Delete>** to remove the subreport from the report layout.

14. Close the report without saving and close the database.

Access 2003   *ECDL/ICDL*   *Section 7 Reports*

Driving Lesson 55 - Calculated Fields: Reports

Park and Read

Summary calculation fields are usually added to reports as part of defining grouping levels, but they can be manually created to obtain any mathematical/statistical information that may be required. Calculations using expressions like **Sum** and **Count** will have different effects depending on where they are added in the report.

Manoeuvres

1. Open the **Houses** database. Click on **Reports** and open the **Property by Type** report in **Design View**.

2. Use **File | Page Setup** to change the page orientation to **Landscape**.

3. Click on the **Sorting and Grouping** button, grouping by **Type of Property** has already been defined. Set the **Group Footer** property for **Type of Property** to **Yes** to include a **Type of Property** footer.

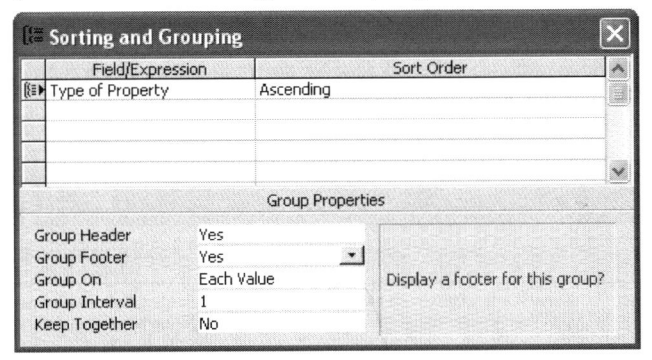

4. Close the **Sorting and Grouping** dialog box.

5. From the **Toolbox** click on the **Text Box** button and click in the **Type of Property Footer**. In the **Unbound** box enter the following calculation: **=Count([Address])**. This will count how many properties are in each group.

6. Change the label to **Number of Properties**.

7. Create another **Text Box** in the **Type of Property Footer**, under the previous box. Resize the footer if necessary. Enter the calculation: **=Avg([Price])**. This will calculate the average price of property per group.

8. View the **Avg([Price])** field property and set the **Format** property to **Currency**, **Decimal Places** to **0** and the label to **Average Price**.

Driving Lesson 55 - Continued

9. To total the price of all properties, create a third text box in the **Type of Property Footer**.

10. Enter the expression: **=Sum([Price])** and set the **Format** property to **Currency**, **Decimal Places** to **0** and the label to **Total Price**.

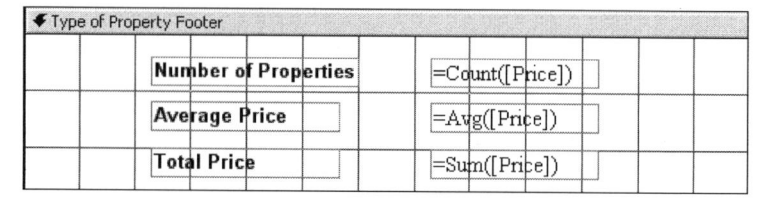

Type of Property Footer		
Number of Properties	=Count([Price])	
Average Price	=Avg([Price])	
Total Price	=Sum([Price])	

11. Switch to **Print Preview** and scroll through the pages to view the calculations.

12. Return to **Design View**. Click and drag a box around the **Count**, **Avg** and **Sum** calculated fields to select them and click on the **Copy** button.

13. Resize the **Report Footer**, click in it, then click on the **Paste** button, to paste the fields into it.

14. Change the field labels in the **Report Footer** to **Total Number of Properties**, **Report Average Price** and **Report Total Price**.

15. Preview the report. At the end of the report are the total number, average price and total price of properties for the entire report.

16. Save and close the report, then close the database.

17. Open the **Computer Shop** database and create a new report in **Design View** using the **Repairs** table. Place all fields on to the **Detail** area.

18. In the **Page Header** create the label **Maximum and Minimum Costs**. Increase the text size to **12pt bold** and resize the label so that the text fits on one line.

19. Select **View | Report Header/Footer** and draw a line at the top of the **Report Footer**.

20. Beneath the line create a text box and enter the following expression: **=Max([Price])**. Format the field as currency and change the label to **Maximum Price**. Select **2** from the **Decimal Places** drop down list.

21. Create a second text box beneath the first and enter the following expression: **=Min([Price])**. Format the field as currency and change the label to **Minimum Price**. Select **2** from the **Decimal Places** drop down list.

Access 2003   ECDL/ICDL   *Section 7 Reports*

Driving Lesson 55 - Continued

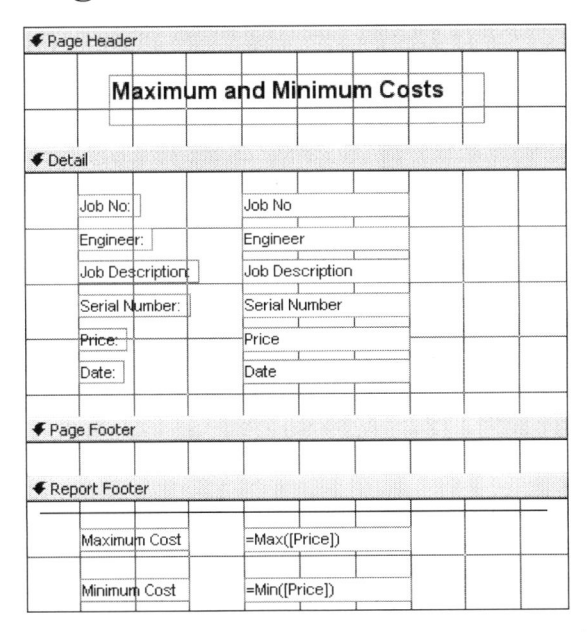

22. Preview the report and scroll to the end to see maximum and minimum costs for all repairs.
23. Save the report as **Max Costs** and close it. Close the database.
24. Calculated fields can also involve text fields. Open the **Staff** database.
25. Open the **Staffing** report in **Design View**. The two name fields can be combined into a single field. This is called **concatenation**.
26. Delete the **Surname** and **First Name** labels and fields.
27. Create a text box in the resulting space and enter the following expression: **=([First Name] & " " & [Surname])**. The space is added in to separate the fields.
28. Change the label to **Name:**, and use **Format Painter** to standardise the format of the new field.

> The **&** symbol is also known as **concatenate**. This is a useful feature in reports, as it tidies up spacing, but beware of using it in forms, as it restricts searching.

29. Preview the report and notice the names are now shown in a single field.
30. Close the report and the database, saving any changes.

Driving Lesson 56 - Calculating Percentages

Park and Read

Calculated fields can be used to show percentages in reports. In particular they can show the value of each detail line as a percentage of the report total.

Manoeuvres

1. Open the **Pets** database and the **Percentage Sold** report in **Design View**. This report contains a record for each sale, including the number of animals sold, and a calculated field in the **Report Footer** to show the total number of animals sold. A calculated field can be added to each detail line to show the number sold as a percentage of the total number sold.

2. Use the **Text Box** button to create a new field to the right of the **Number Sold** field in the detail area.

3. Click and drag the new label box to the right of the **Unbound** box and enter the text '**of the total**'. Adjust the positions as shown below.

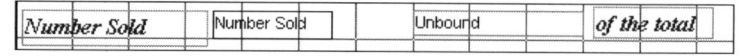

4. Right click on the **Unbound** box and select **Properties** from the shortcut menu, then the **Data** tab.

5. In **Control Source**, enter the calculation: **=[Number Sold] / [Text12]** (**Text12** is the name of the **Report Total** field in the **Report Footer**). This is an alternative to typing the calculation directly into the unbound box.

If a report has grouped subtotals, percentages can be calculated as a percentage of the group totals instead of report totals, or they can be placed in the group footer to give group totals as a percentage of report totals.

6. Set the **Format** property to **Percent** from the drop down list.

7. Close the **Properties** and switch to **Print Preview**.

8. The calculated percentage field shows that the 9 cats sold in this sale represent 6.87% of the total number of animals sold (if Driving Lesson 39 has not been completed, this value may be 25.00%).

9. Save and close the **Percentage Sold** report then close the **Pets** database.

Driving Lesson 57 - Report Headers & Footers

Park and Read

Reports can have header and footer areas defined. Group headers and footers are defined with grouping levels. Report headers and footers appear at the beginning and end of every report. Page headers and footers are printed at the top and bottom of every printed page. Data fields can be added to header and footer areas. These can include fields from the field list or the date and time. Automatic page numbering can be added to page headers or footers.

Manoeuvres

1. Open the **Houses** database and the view the **Sample1** report.

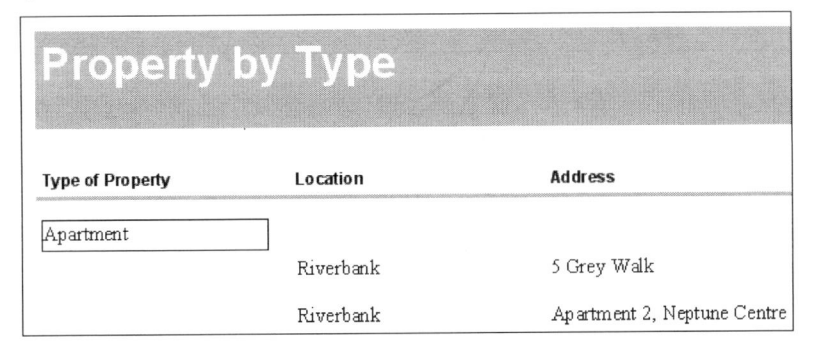

2. Look at page 2. The group has overflowed a page and there is no group heading on the second page.

3. Switch to **Design View**. Click and drag the **Type of Property** field straight upwards from the **Type of Property Header** to the **Page Header**, above the existing label.

4. View the report again. As the field is now in the **Page Header** it appears on every page.

5. Switch to **Design View**. With the **Type of Property** field selected, select **Edit | Copy**.

6. Click in the **Type of Property Footer** area and select **Edit | Paste**.

7. Delete the **Group Total** label in this area and move the **Type of Property** field to take its place.

8. Paste the **Type of Property** field again, this time into the **Page Footer** area. Move it just to the right of the current date field.

Driving Lesson 57 - Continued

9. View the report and look at page 2. The **Type of Property** field now appears in three places.

10. Switch to **Design View** and click on the **Type of Property** field in the **Page Footer**. Press <Delete> to remove it.

11. If a field was common throughout the whole report it could also be placed in **Report Header** or **Report Footer** in the same way. It is more common however to insert fields such as **Date**, **Time**, **Page Numbers** and **Labels**.

12. To insert a date and time field in the header, click in the **Report Header** and select **Insert | Date and Time**.

13. Select any date and time options and click **OK**. Move the fields to the right of the **Report Header** area.

14. Click in the **Page Footer** and select **Insert | Page Numbers**.

15. Select the options below:

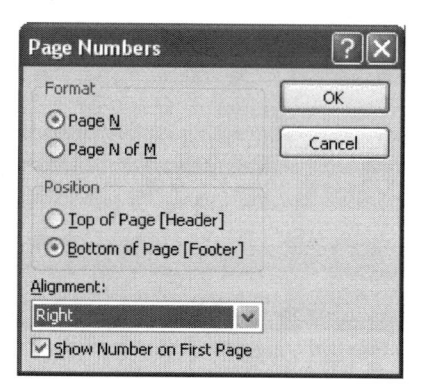

16. Click **OK**.

17. Use the **Label** tool, , to draw a label in the centre of the **Page Footer**.

18. Type your name in the label.

19. Preview the report to see the information which has been added to the header and footer.

20. Leave the report open.

Driving Lesson 58 - Printing Reports

Park and Read

It is possible to print out reports, either to show all pages, a selected page, or a range of pages.

Manoeuvres

1. With the **Sample1** report open select **File | Print**.
2. From **Print Range** select **All**.

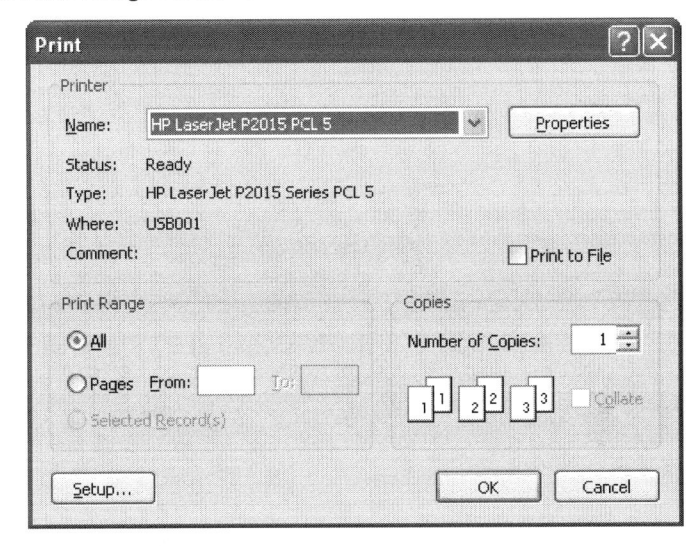

*A range of pages or an individual page, can be printed using the **Pages** option in **Print Range** and the number of copies can be specified at the right of the dialog box in the **Copies** area.*

3. Click **OK** to print the entire report.
4. Close the report without saving and close the database.

Driving Lesson 59 - Revision

This is not an ECDL test. Testing may only be carried out through certified ECDL test centres. This covers the features introduced in this section. Try not to refer to the preceding Driving Lessons while completing it.

1. Open the **Supermarket** database.
2. Use **Report Wizard** to create a report based on the **Stock** table.
3. Show all available fields and group the report by **Category**.
4. Include **Min** and **Max** summary values for **Price**.
5. Use a **Stepped** layout, **Landscape** orientation and **Corporate** style.
6. Name the report **Stock List**.
7. In **Design View** create **Calculated Fields** to display the **Average Price** of the items in each category and for the whole report.
8. Label the fields **Category Average** and **Report Average** respectively.
9. Format all price fields as **Currency**.
10. Print the report.
11. Close the report and the database, saving any changes.

If you experienced any difficulty completing the Revision, refer back to the Driving Lessons in this section. Then redo the Revision.

Driving Lesson 60 - Revision

This is not an ECDL test. Testing may only be carried out through certified ECDL test centres. This covers the features introduced in this section. Try not to refer to the preceding Driving Lessons while completing it.

1. Use the **Country** database.

2. Create a query to find all of the countries with a population over 30 million.

Populations in this table are recorded in millions.

3. Use the results to produce a report displaying the following fields in the order specified: **Region**, **Country** and **Population**. Make the report stepped, grouped by **Region** and sorted in descending order of **Population**.

4. Give the report the title: **Highly Populated**.

5. Display the total and average population for each region. Insert the description **Total Population for this Region** alongside the total figure, and, insert the description **Average Population for this Region** alongside the average figure.

6. Change the **Format** properties of the total and average fields to **Fixed** with **0** decimal places (integers).

7. Add a calculated field to the detail (Country) record to show the population for that country as a percentage of the **Total Population** for that **Region**.

8. Print the report in portrait orientation with no page numbers and no date. Ensure all field headings and records are fully displayed.

9. Save and close the report.

10. Close the **Country** database.

If you experienced any difficulty completing the Revision, refer back to the Driving Lessons in this section. Then redo the Revision.

Once you are confident with the features, complete the Record of Achievement Matrix referring to the section at the end of the guide. Only when competent move on to the next Section.

Section 8
Import and Link Data

By the end of this Section you should be able to:

> **Import Data from Spreadsheets**
>
> **Import Data from Text Files**
>
> **Import Data from Tables**
>
> **Link a Database to External Data**

To gain an understanding of the above features, work through the **Driving Lessons** in this **Section**.

For each **Driving Lesson**, read the **Park and Read** instructions, without touching the keyboard, then work through the numbered steps of the **Manoeuvres** on the computer. Complete the **Revision Exercise(s)** at the end of the section to test your knowledge.

Driving Lesson 61 - Importing Spreadsheets

Park and Read

It is possible to **import** data from one database to another or from a different type of file such as spreadsheet or text file. This can be very useful if the data required for an *Access* application already exists in another location, either in a different database or in an *Excel* spreadsheet for example. Importing converts the source data format and creates a new copy of the data within *Access*. The data can be then edited in *Access,* and is completely independent of the source. This allows much greater flexibility for data entry.

Manoeuvres

1. Open the **Contacts** database. From the **Database Window** select **File | Get External Data | Import**.

2. At the **Import** dialog box select the folder where the data is stored and change the **Files of type** to **Microsoft Excel**. Select the **Sick** file and click **Import**.

3. After a few seconds the **Import Spreadsheet Wizard** appears. Specify that the **First Row Contains Column Headings**.

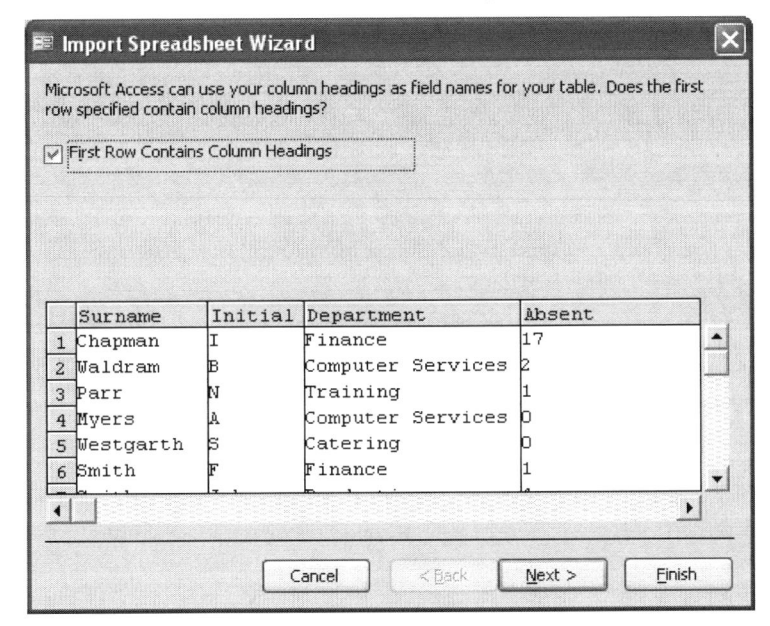

Driving Lesson 61 - Continued

4. Click **Next**. Specify to store the data **In a New Table**.

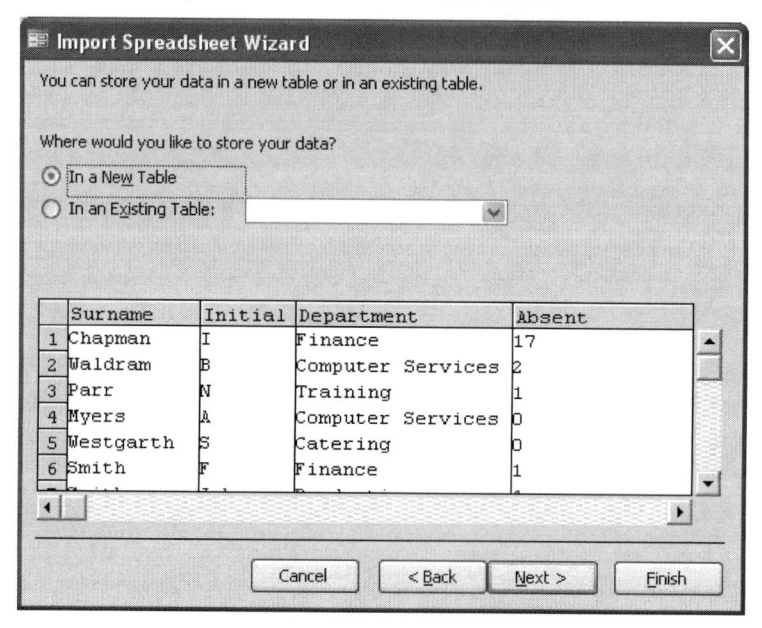

> Notice there is an option to import the data into an existing table. This will add records to the end of the table, but great care must be taken so that the format of the imported data <u>exactly</u> matches the format of the existing table, or the import will fail.

5. Click **Next**. There are options here to change the names of any field or to choose to omit certain fields from the import process. Take no action but click **Next** again.

6. There are options on this screen to define one of the input fields as the **Primary Key** for the table or to allow *Access* to add a new field (a sequential number field) as the **Primary Key**. Select the third option, **No primary key** and click **Next**.

7. Call the table **Sick List** and click **Finish** to create it. Click **OK** at the **Finished Importing** message.

8. Open the table to view the data and adjust the column widths if necessary.

9. Save the table and close it but leave the database open.

Driving Lesson 62 - Importing Text Files

Park and Read

It is also possible to import text data into a database. The text file can be in any basic text format such as **.txt** (text) or **.csv** (comma separated variables).

Manoeuvres

1. With the **Contacts** database still open, select **File | Get External Data | Import**.

2. From the **Import** dialog box select the location of the supplied data folder and change **Files of type** to **Text Files [*.txt; *.csv; *.tab; *.asc]**. Select the **tourists.csv** file and click **Import**.

3. From the **Import Text Wizard** select **Delimited**.

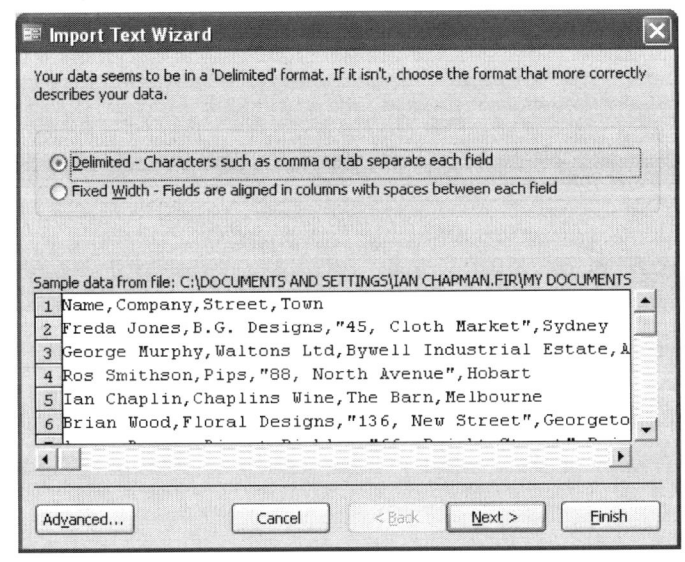

4. Click **Next** and select **Comma** as the **Delimiter**. Select quotes (") as the **Text Qualifier** (all text within quotes will then be treated as a single field).

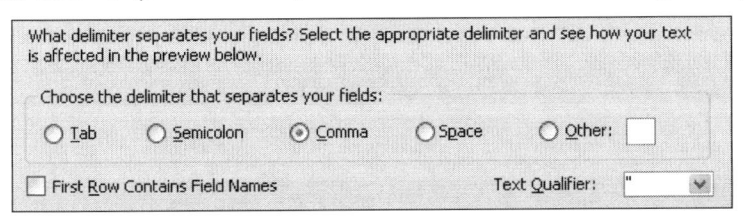

Driving Lesson 62 - Continued

> The data in the source file must be divided into individual fields by a delimiter of some form. The Delimiter character will vary depending on the type of text file being imported. It is **Comma** for **.csv** files, and is often **Tab** for a table in a **.txt** file. Check the source file if necessary to establish the delimiter.

5. Check **First Row Contains Field Names** and click **Next**.

6. Select **In a New Table**, then click **Next** and **Next** again.

7. Choose **No primary key** and click **Next**.

8. Call the table **Tourist List** and click **Finish**, selecting **OK** at the prompt.

9. View the new table, adjust the column widths where necessary, then save and close it.

10. Following the steps above, import the text file **Colleagues.txt** into a new table called **Holiday List**. It is separated by **Tab Delimiter**.

> Files in various formats, e.g. Paradox and dBASE can be imported into an Access database. XML files can also be imported - this is a type of language particularly suited to the Internet and helps information systems share structural data. Select the correct **File Type** from the **Import** dialog box and follow the **Import Wizard** steps.

11. Leave the database open for the next Driving Lesson.

Driving Lesson 63 - Importing Tables

Park and Read

Importing data from a table in another database is very simple as the data is already in the correct format.

Manoeuvres

1. With the **Contacts** database still open, select **File | Get External Data | Import**.

2. From the **Import** dialog box select the location of the supplied data folder and change **Files of type** to **Microsoft Access**.

3. Select the **CiA** database and click **Import**. Make sure the **Tables** tab is selected.

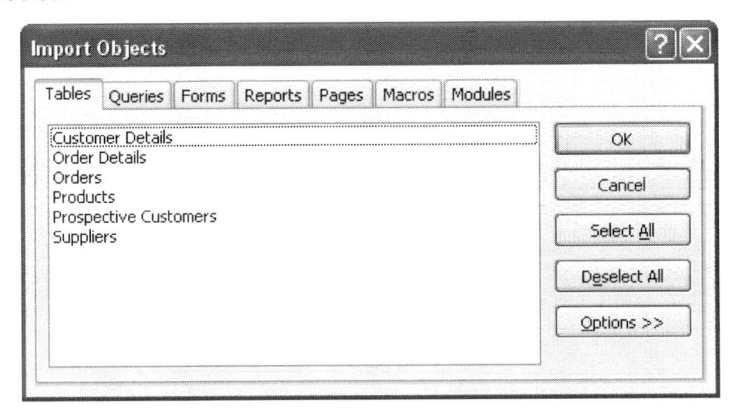

> The **Junction** table may also be present (from Driving Lesson 26).

4. Select the **Suppliers** table.

> Any object can be imported, but there is no point importing a **Form** or a **Report** for example, unless the matching tables were present.

5. Click **OK**. The table is imported into the **Contacts** database.

6. Open the **Suppliers** table in **Design View** then **Datasheet View**. All formatting and data has been copied.

> This is a separate copy of the table, completely independent of the original.

7. Close the table and the database.

Driving Lesson 64 - Linking Data

Park and Read

Linking involves creating a database table from an external source without creating a separate copy of the object source within the database.

Any changes to the source file are automatically reflected in the database. Content or design changes <u>cannot</u> be made directly to the table in the database.

A disadvantage is that if the source file is ever moved or deleted, the database table will no longer be available.

Manoeuvres

1. Open the **CiA** database and select **File | Get External Data | Link Tables**.

2. In the **Link** dialog box, change **Files of type** to **Microsoft Excel** and make sure **Look in** shows the location of the supplied data.

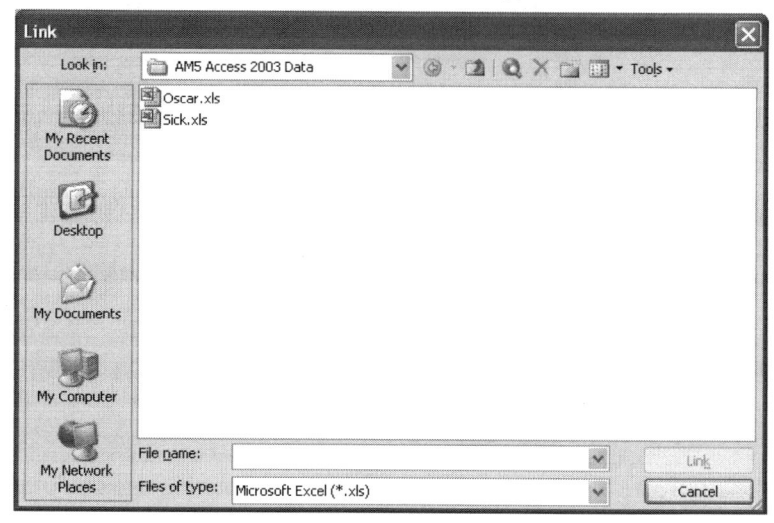

3. Select the file **Sick.xls** and click **Link**.

*External data in various formats, as in the last two Driving Lessons, can be linked to a database. This includes text files (**.txt**), comma separated variable files (**.csv**) and various database formats. The process is always the same; select the correct format from files of type in the **Link** dialog box and follow the Wizard steps.*

Driving Lesson 64 - Continued

4. When the **Link Spreadsheet Wizard** is displayed check the **First Row Contains Column Headings** box and click **Next**.

5. Name the table **Linked Absence** and click **Finish**. Click **OK** at the prompt.

6. The new table is shown in the **Database Window** as, [Linked Absence icon]. This indicates that it is linked to information from *Excel*. Double click on the icon to open the table. No data can be amended.

7. Switch to **Design View**. A warning message will be displayed. Read the message then click **No**. Close the **Linked Absence** table.

8. Open *Excel* and the **Sick** workbook. Change the number of days' absence for **I Chapman** to **34**, save the workbook and close *Excel*.

9. Open the **Linked Absence** table from the **CiA** database to see the changes made in *Excel* have been applied here.

10. Close the table and use *Windows Explorer* or some other means, to rename **Sick.xls** as **Sickcopy.xls**.

11. Try and open the **Linked Absence** table from the **CiA** database again. This will not be allowed now because *Access* can no longer find the source file **Sick.xls**. Click **OK** at the error message.

12. To link to a database table select **File | Get External Data | Link Tables**.

13. From the **Import** dialog box select the location of the supplied data folder and change **Files of type** to **Microsoft Access**.

14. Select the **Staff** database and click **Link**.

15. Select the **Staff List** table and click **OK**. **Staff List** is added to the database as a **Linked Table**.

16. Open the table in **Datasheet View**. The link is now 'two way'. Data changes can be made here and will be applied to the original table. Design changes still cannot be made.

17. Close the table and the database.

18. Rename **Sickcopy** back to **Sick**.

19. Leave *Access* open but close all other open applications.

Driving Lesson 65 - Revision

This is not an ECDL test. Testing may only be carried out through certified ECDL test centres. This covers the features introduced in this section. Try not to refer to the preceding Driving Lessons while completing it.

1. Create a new database called **Awards**.
2. Import data from the *Microsoft Excel* file **Oscar**.
3. On the first Wizard screen click the option for **First Row Contains Column Headings**. There is a message that some of the column headings cannot be used as *Access* field names. Click **OK** to continue.
4. Create a new table for the data and accept all fields.
5. Choose the **Year** field as your own primary key and name the table **Oscar**.
6. Examine the **Oscar** table in *Access*. Look at the field names in the column headings. Some of them were supplied by *Access* rather than taken from the spreadsheet. By examining the original **Oscar** spreadsheet file in *Excel*, explain why the original column headings could not be used.
7. Close the table and the database, saving any changes.
8. Close *Excel*.

See the **Answers** section at the back of the guide.

If you experienced any difficulty completing the Revision, refer back to the Driving Lessons in this section. Then redo the Revision.

Access 2003　　　　　　　　ECDL/ICDL　　　　Section 8 Import and Link Data

Driving Lesson 66 - Revision

This is not an ECDL test. Testing may only be carried out through certified ECDL test centres. This covers the features introduced in this section. Try not to refer to the preceding Driving Lessons while completing it.

1. Open the **Custom Computers** database.

2. Import the **Staff List** table from the **Personnel** database as a **Linked** table.

3. In the **Custom Computers** database create a new summary query based on data from the linked **Staff List** table to sum the salaries for all staff. Make a note of the total value.

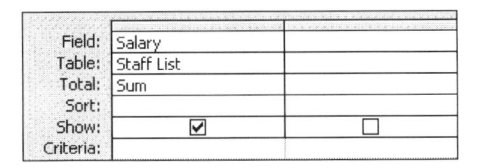

Field:	Salary	
Table:	Staff List	
Total:	Sum	
Sort:		
Show:	☑	☐
Criteria:		

4. Save the query as **Salary** and close it.

5. Open the **Personnel** database and the **Staff List** table.

6. Change the salary for the first record (**Peter Nyder**) to **£28,000**.

7. Close the table.

8. Open the **Custom Computers** database and run the **Salary** query. What is the new total?

9. Close the query and database.

See the **Answers** section at the back of the guide.

If you experienced any difficulty completing the Revision, refer back to the Driving Lessons in this section. Then redo the Revision.

Once you are confident with the features, complete the Record of Achievement Matrix referring to the section at the end of the guide. Only when competent move on to the next Section.

Section 9
Action Queries

By the end of this Section you should be able to:

>Create Append Queries
>
>Create Delete Queries
>
>Make a Table from a Query
>
>Create an Update Query

To gain an understanding of the above features, work through the **Driving Lessons** in this **Section**.

For each **Driving Lesson**, read the **Park and Read** instructions, without touching the keyboard, then work through the numbered steps of the **Manoeuvres** on the computer. Complete the **Revision Exercise(s)** at the end of the section to test your knowledge.

Driving Lesson 67 - Append Query

Park and Read

An **Append Query** selects a group of records from one table using all the features of a query, and adds them to the end of another table. Note that the information is not removed from the original table.

Manoeuvres

1. Open the **CiA** database.

2. Select **Queries** and click on **New** and start a new query in **Design View**. This query will search the **Prospective Customers** table and select those records with a status of **A** (**Status = A**, indicates **Prospective** customers who have now become **Actual** customers). These records will be automatically added to the **Customer Details** table.

3. From the **Show Table** dialog box choose the **Prospective Customers** table. Click **Add** and **Close**.

4. Click the down arrow on the **Query Type** button, and select **Append Query**. The **Append** dialog box appears.

5. From **Table Name** select **Customer Details** as the table to which the records are to be added.

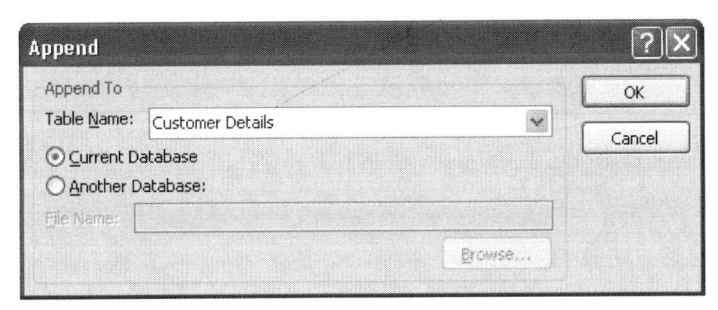

6. Click **OK**. A new row appears on the query grid, **Append To**:

7. Place the **Customer Ref** field on to the grid. Notice **Append To** also contains **Customer Ref**. This is the **Customer Ref** field in the **Customer Details** table.

8. Place the following fields on to the grid: **Title**, **First Name**, **Surname**, **Company**, **Address**, **County**, **Telephone**, **Fax**, **Information** and **Status**.

Driving Lesson 67 - Continued

9. Each field on the grid has an **Append To** value, indicating the field on the new table to which it will go. The **Status** field has no **Append To** value because there is no matching field on the **Customer Details** table Leaving the **Append To** value blank means that the field will not be included in the append.

10. The field is however used in the selection process. In the **Status** column, enter **A** in **Criteria**.

11. To view the information that is to be appended without actually appending it, click on the **Datasheet** button, , prior to **Run**. This will show the records that will be appended.

12. Return to the **Query Design**. Click **Run**, , from the toolbar.

13. A dialog box appears stating how many records will be appended.

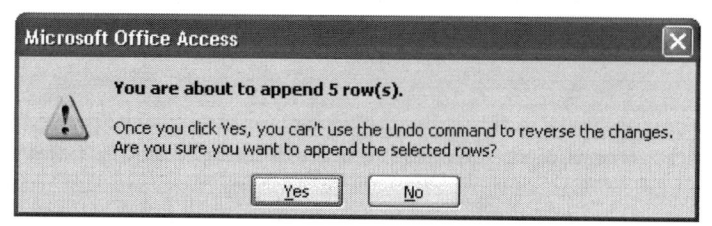

14. Click **Yes** to append the records to the stated table.

Records which are appended are not deleted from the source table. The 5 records added here still exist on the Prospective Customers table.

15. Save the query as **Append New Customers**. The query can now be run whenever required and will take any records flagged as new customers and add them to the **Customer Details** table.

16. Close the query and open up the **Customer Details** table to view the appended records (the first 5).

17. Close the table but leave the database open for the next Driving Lesson.

Access 2003   ECDL/ICDL   Section 9 Action Queries

Driving Lesson 68 - Delete Query

Park and Read

A **Delete Query** will delete a selected group of records from one or more tables. This could be run after an **Append** query for example, to remove all the updated records from the original table.

Manoeuvres

1. With the **CiA** database still open, start a new query in **Design View**.

2. Add the **Prospective Customers** table to the query grid and close the **Show Table** dialog box.

3. Choose the **Delete Query** option, [Delete Query], from the **Query Type** drop down menu.

4. Add **Customer Ref, Company** and **Status** to the grid and specify the **Criteria** as **A** in the **Status** field.

Field:	Customer Ref	Company	Status
Table:	Prospective Customers	Prospective Customers	Prospective Customers
Sort:			
Show:	✓	✓	✓
Criteria:			"A"
or:			

5. Click the **Datasheet** button to view the records that will be deleted. These are the same records that were appended to the **Customer Details** table.

> Any number of fields can be added to the grid to view exactly which records are selected, but it is the <u>whole</u> record that will always be deleted.

6. Return to **Design View** and **Run** the query.

7. Click **Yes** to confirm the deletion, then save the query as **Delete Appended Records** and close it.

8. Open the **Prospective Customers** table. All the customers whose **Status** was **A** should now be deleted.

> Delete queries can be modified in **Design View**, like any other query.

9. Close the table but leave the database open for the next Driving Lesson.

Module AM5 Database Advanced Level   121   © CiA Training Ltd 2009

Driving Lesson 69 - Make-Table Query

Park and Read

A **Make-Table Query** selects data from one or more tables, using all the features of a query, and creates a new table from that data. Not all the fields from the original table(s) need to be included in the new table.

Manoeuvres

1. A table is to be made containing all the unpaid orders. From the **CiA** database start a new query in **Design View** and add the **Customer Details** and **Orders** tables to the query grid.

2. Choose the **Make-Table Query** option, `Make-Table Query...`, from the **Query Type** drop down menu.

3. At the dialog box enter the **Table Name** as **Unpaid Orders**.

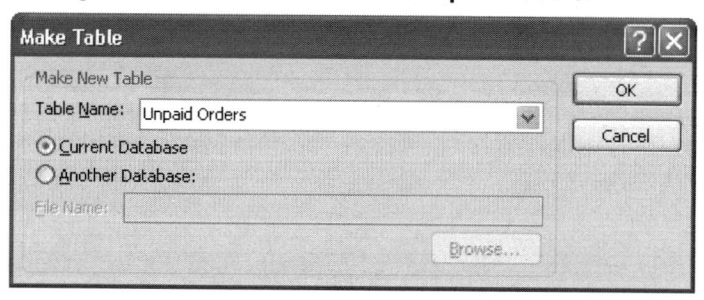

4. Click **OK**. From **Customer Details** place the **Title**, **First Name**, **Surname**, **Company** and **Telephone** fields on to the grid. From **Orders**, place the **Order Ref**, **Order Date** and **Paid** fields on to the grid.

5. Specify the **Criteria** for **Paid** as **No**. Uncheck the **Show** box for **Paid**, this means that this field will not be included in the new records.

6. **Run** the query. Select **Yes** at the dialog box.

7. Save the query and name it **Make Unpaid Orders Table**. Close it.

Driving Lesson 69 - Continued

8. Open the **Unpaid Orders** table to view the data. This table has been created to hold details of all orders which are currently unpaid.

9. Close the table and open the **Make Unpaid Orders Table** query in **Design View**.

10. The query is to be modified. Delete the **First Name** from the query grid.

11. Save and run the query.

12. There is a prompt that the existing table will be deleted. Click **Yes** and then **Yes** again at the next prompt.

13. Close the query.

14. View the **Unpaid Orders** table. Notice that the **First Name** field has been removed.

15. Close the table but leave the database open.

Driving Lesson 70 - Update Query

Park and Read

An **Update Query** will update a specific field within a table(s). For example, increasing all prices by 10%, changing a name of a product, etc.

Manoeuvres

1. From the **CiA** database, open the **Products** table and note the prices of the first 5 items. Close the table and start a new query in **Design View** based on the **Products** table.

2. From the **Query Type** button select **Update Query**.

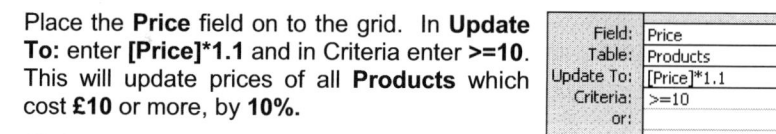

3. Place the **Price** field on to the grid. In **Update To:** enter **[Price]*1.1** and in Criteria enter **>=10**. This will update prices of all **Products** which cost **£10** or more, by **10%**.

4. Click the **Datasheet** button to view the data that will be updated.

5. Return to **Design View** and **Run** the query.

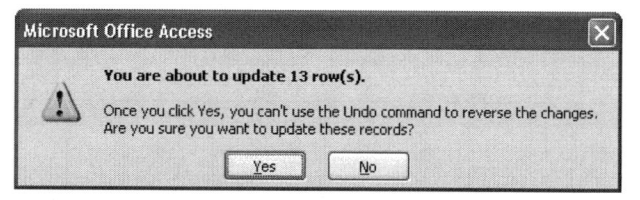

6. Click **Yes** at the update prompt.

7. Save the query as **Update Prices** and close it.

8. Open the **Products** table again and view the updated prices for the first five records. All prices for products that used to cost £10 or more are now increased by **10%**.

9. Close the table and view the query in **Design View**. There's been a management decision to increase those prices by a further **5%**.

10. Change the calculation to **[Price]*1.05** and run the query again, clicking **Yes** at the prompt.

11. Save and close the query and open the **Products** table to check the modified prices.

12. Close the database.

See the **Answers** section at the back of the guide.

Driving Lesson 71 - Revision

This is not an ECDL test. Testing may only be carried out through certified ECDL test centres. This covers the features introduced in this section. Try not to refer to the preceding Driving Lessons while completing it.

1. Open the **Transport** database.

2. Create a **Make-Table** query containing all the fields from the **Buses** table.

3. Set the criteria to only pick out Buses whose number of **Journeys** is **4**. Call the query **4journeys** and the table **Top Routes**.

4. Using an **Append** query, add all the records from the **Buses** table whose number of **Journeys** is **3,** to the **Top Routes** table. Call the query **3journeys**.

5. Create a query to delete any bus from the **Top Routes** table whose **Size** is **Mini**, calling the query **Delete Minis**.

6. Create an **Update** query called **Change Name** to change all **Size** values of **Single** to **Coach** in the **Top Routes** table.

7. Close all the objects and the database.

If you experienced any difficulty completing the Revision, refer back to the Driving Lessons in this section. Then redo the Revision.

Driving Lesson 72 - Revision

This is not an ECDL test. Testing may only be carried out through certified ECDL test centres. This covers the features introduced in this section. Try not to refer to the preceding Driving Lessons while completing it.

1. Open the **Sales** database. Bill Anderson has retired. His position is to be filled by Phil Smith.
2. Create an **Update Query** to make the change. Select the **Sales Figures** table. Place the **Area** and **Manager** fields on to the grid.
3. For the **Area Criteria**, enter **Northern**.
4. For **Update To** in the **Manager** field, enter **Phil Smith**.
5. Save the query as **Northern Replacement**.
6. Run the query and view the changes to the **Sales Figures** table.
7. Use a **Make Table Query** to create a new table containing any sales above **£15,000**.
8. Name the new table **Top Ten**.
9. Select the **Sales Figures** table and add the **Last Name**, **Area** and **Sales** fields to the grid.
10. For the **Sales Criteria**, enter **>15000** and save the query as **Top Sales**.
11. Run the query, then close it.
12. Open the **Top Ten** table.
13. Which area includes the highest sales value?
14. Who is the salesperson with the highest sales for the **Eastern** region?
15. Close the table and the database.

See the **Answers** section at the back of the guide.

If you experienced any difficulty completing the Revision, refer back to the Driving Lessons in this section. Then redo the Revision.

Once you are confident with the features, complete the Record of Achievement Matrix referring to the section at the end of the guide. Only when competent move on to the next Section.

Section 10
Query Wizards

By the end of this Section you should be able to:

> Create a Crosstab Query
>
> Create a Find Duplicates Query
>
> Create a Find Unmatched Query

To gain an understanding of the above features, work through the **Driving Lessons** in this **Section**.

For each **Driving Lesson**, read the **Park and Read** instructions, without touching the keyboard, then work through the numbered steps of the **Manoeuvres** on the computer. Complete the **Revision Exercise(s)** at the end of the section to test your knowledge.

Driving Lesson 73 - Crosstab Query

Park and Read

By default, a line on a query result represents a record of some kind. A **Crosstab Query** however shows summarised values such as **Sum**, **Avg**, **Count**, **Max**, **Min**, etc. for fields within a table or query and groups them together into a matrix type of display. The columns and rows of the matrix can be any fields from the table or query. Crosstab queries can either be created via the wizard or manually. It is recommended to use the wizard.

Manoeuvres

1. Open the **CiA** database and create a query to include the following tables and fields.

Customer Details	Orders	Order Details	Products
Company		Amount	Product

   Even though there are no fields placed on to the query grid from the **Orders** table, it needs to be included in the query to maintain the relationships between all the other tables.

2. Save the query as **Product Info** and close it.

3. From **Queries** select **New** and then **Crosstab Query Wizard**. Click **OK**.

4. Choose the **Queries** option from **View**, then select **Product Info** as the source of the data for this crosstab query.

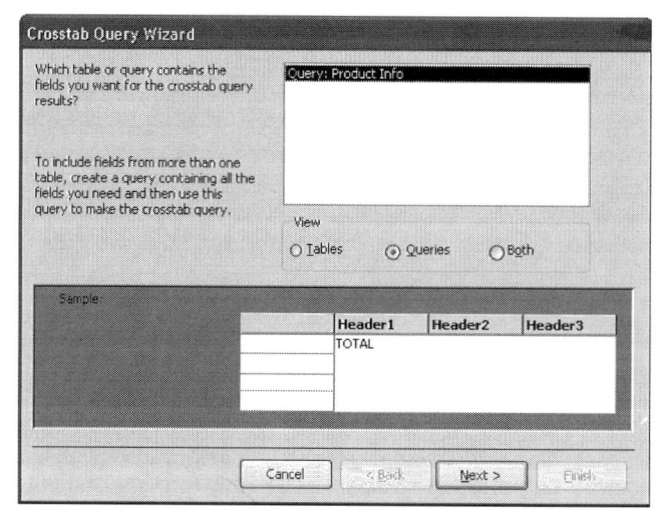

Driving Lesson 73 - Continued

5. Click **Next**. Click on **Company** then [>] to select that field for the **row headings**.

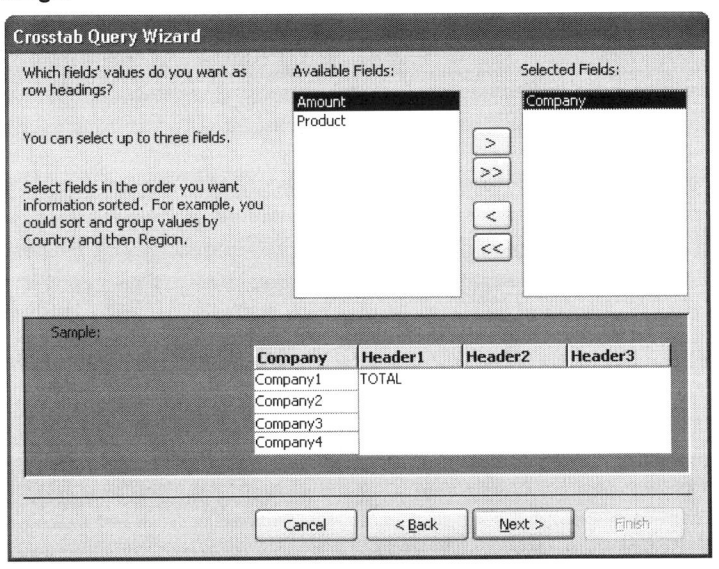

6. Notice that the lower half of each wizard screen shows a sample of the final query, as far as it has been defined. Click **Next** then select **Product** to specify that for the **column headings**.

7. Click **Next**. Select the **Amount** field, then the **Sum** calculation.

8. Click **Next**.

9. Name the query **Product Info Results**.

10. Click **Finish** to view the results. The query is a grid of the total amount of products each company has bought.

11. To modify the query, go to **Design View**. Click in the **Sort** field for **Company** and select **Ascending**.

12. Save and run the query.

13. Notice how the results are now sorted alphabetically by **Company**.

14. Close the query but leave the database open.

Driving Lesson 74 - Find Duplicates Query

Park and Read

A **Find Duplicates Query** will search a table for records where individual fields have duplicate values. For example, company details that may have been entered twice by mistake.

Manoeuvres

1. A query is to be created to find companies who appear more than once in the database. From the **CiA** database select **Queries** and click **New**.

2. Select the **Find Duplicates Query Wizard** and click **OK**. Choose the **Customer Details** table and click **Next**.

3. Select the **Company** field then click [>], select the **Address** field then click [>] again.

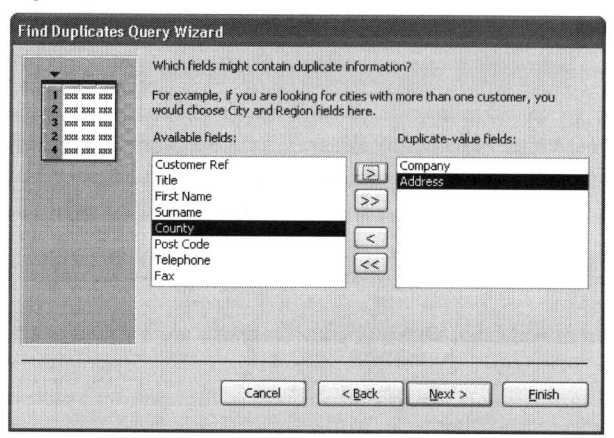

4. By selecting two fields here, both fields must match before records will be selected as duplicates. In this example, two records with the same **Company** name but different **Address** fields will <u>not</u> be selected as duplicates. Click **Next**.

5. Click [>>] to show all the fields in the query results then click **Next**.

6. Finally, name the query **Duplicate Company Details**.

7. Click **Finish**. The results contain the details of the companies that appear more than once with the same address in the **Customer Details** table.

8. Switch to **Design View** to modify the query. Remove the **Fax** field from the query grid. Save the query and view the changes.

9. Close the query but leave the database open.

Driving Lesson 75 - Find Unmatched Query

Park and Read

The **Find Unmatched Query** will find records in one table that do not have a matching record in another table. For example, **Customers** who do not have any records on an **Orders** table or **Students** with no records on a **Courses** table.

Manoeuvres

1. A query is to be created to find all the companies who have not made any orders. From the **CiA** database select **Queries**.

2. Click **New** then **Find Unmatched Query Wizard**. Click **OK**.

3. Select the **Customer Details** table as the table that contains the information. Click **Next**.

4. Select the **Orders** table as the table that is to be searched. Click **Next**.

5. Highlight the **Customer Ref** in both tables and click <=>.

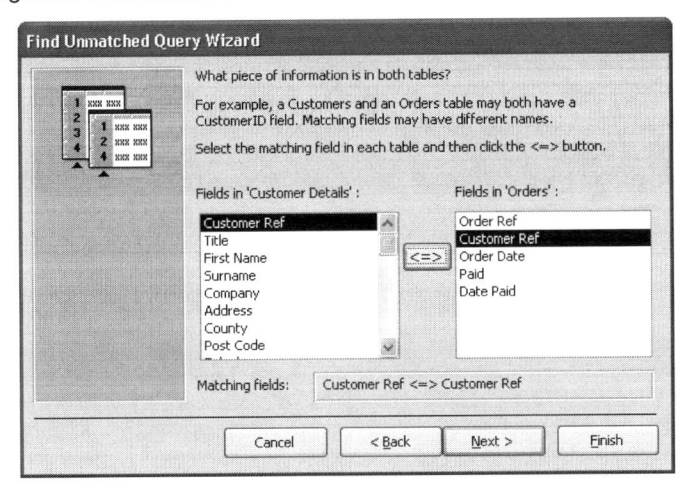

6. This is the field that is to be matched in both tables. Click **Next**.

7. Click >>, to view all the fields in the query results. Click **Next**.

8. Name the query **No Orders** and click **Finish** to view the results. A list of all the customers who have not placed any orders appears.

> To modify a **Find Unmatched** query, make the changes in **Design View**. If major changes are required, it may be better to create a new query.

9. Close the query and the database.

Driving Lesson 76 - Revision

This is not an ECDL test. Testing may only be carried out through certified ECDL test centres. This covers the features introduced in this section. Try not to refer to the preceding Driving Lessons while completing it.

1. Open the **Premises** database.
2. Use the wizard to create a query which will display all the properties which have exactly the same price as another property on the **Commercial** table.
3. As well as **Price**, show the fields **Property Ref**, **Location** and **Address**.
4. Call the query **Same Price**.
5. Close the query.
6. Use the wizard to create a **Crosstab** query which shows the total number of each **Type** of premises in each **Location**.
7. Name it **Properties**.
8. Close the query and the database.

If you experienced any difficulty completing the Revision, refer back to the Driving Lessons in this section. Then redo the Revision.

Once you are confident with the features, complete the Record of Achievement Matrix referring to the section at the end of the guide. Only when competent move on to the next Section.

Section 11
Macros

By the end of this Section you should be able to:

>Understand Macro Actions
>
>Create a Macro
>
>Attach a Macro to a Control or Object
>
>Create Macros from Controls
>
>Create Command Button Macros

To gain an understanding of the above features, work through the **Driving Lessons** in this **Section**.

For each **Driving Lesson**, read the **Park and Read** instructions, without touching the keyboard, then work through the numbered steps of the **Manoeuvres** on the computer. Complete the **Revision Exercise(s)** at the end of the section to test your knowledge.

Section 11 Macros ECDL/ICDL Access 2003

Driving Lesson 77 - Create a New Macro

Park and Read

A macro is another object in *Access*. Macros are created by selecting an **Action** or **Actions** which will be run when the macro is activated. Some actions require further **Action Arguments** to be specified which control the operation of each action. For example, an **Open Form** macro can be created to open a specified form. **Action Arguments** must be set up to state which form is to be opened and if the form is to be viewed in **Form**, **Design** or **Datasheet View**.

Once created, a macro can be run manually or more commonly, attached to a control on a form.

Manoeuvres

1. Open the **Transport** database. Select **Macros** and click **New** to start a new macro. The **Macro** window appears.

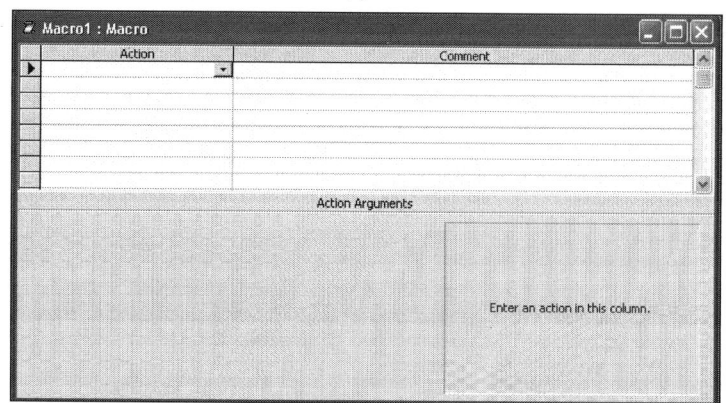

2. Click in the **Action** column and from the drop down arrow, select **OpenForm**.

3. In the **Comment** column enter **Open the Servicing form**.

4. An **Action Arguments** window is displayed at the bottom of the page. Click in **Form Name** and choose the name of the form that is to be opened – **Servicing**. Leave the **View** argument as **Form**. This defines the view that will be used when the form is opened.

Driving Lesson 77 - Continued

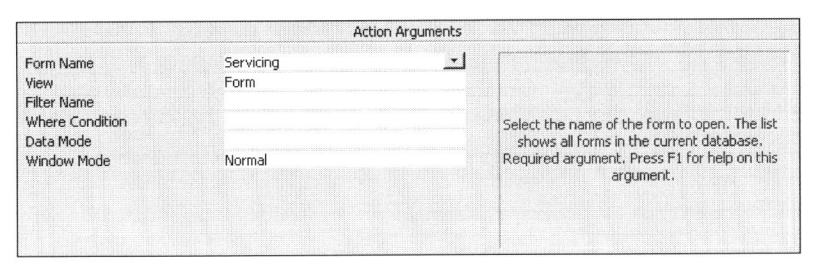

Action Arguments		
Form Name	Servicing	
View	Form	
Filter Name		Select the name of the form to open. The list shows all forms in the current database. Required argument. Press F1 for help on this argument.
Where Condition		
Data Mode		
Window Mode	Normal	

5. Select **Minimize** as an action on the line below the **OpenForm** action. This is a simple function to minimise the display and has no **Arguments**.

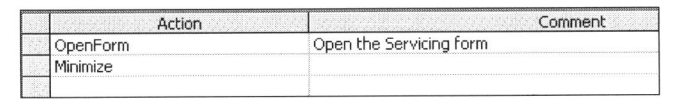

Action	Comment
OpenForm	Open the Servicing form
Minimize	

6. Select **File |Save As** and save the macro as **OpenServicing**.

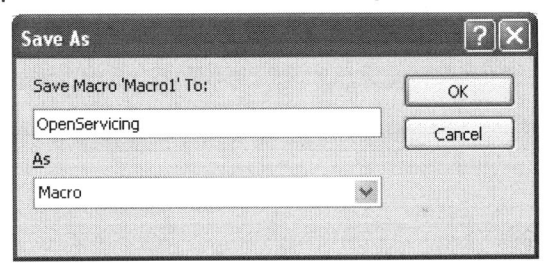

Save As dialog:
Save Macro 'Macro1' To:
OpenServicing
As
Macro

7. Click **OK** and close the **Macro** window.

8. From the **Database Window**, double click the **OpenServicing** macro. The **Servicing** form opens and is minimised.

9. Click the **Servicing** form on the **Task Bar** to display it then close it.

10. Open the **OpenServicing** macro in **Design View**. On the second line, select the **Maximize** action in place of **Minimize**.

11. Save the macro and close it.

12. Double click the **OpenServicing** macro to run it. The **Servicing** form opens and is maximised.

13. Close the form but leave the database open.

Driving Lesson 78 - Attaching a Macro to a Control

Park and Read

Once a macro has been created, it can be attached to various controls on a form, such as a data field, image or command button. It can also be attached to the whole form.

When it has been attached, an **Event** needs to be set up in the properties of the control. This defines what will cause the macro to run, e.g. on a single or double click of the mouse, or when the field is updated, or the when the form is opened. The possible events will vary with the type of control.

Manoeuvres

1. In the **Transport** database, create a new macro. The first action is **Close**. By default it will close the current window. Set the **Save** argument to **No**.

2. The second action is **OpenForm**, with a **Form Name** of **Servicing**.

Action	Comment
Close	Closes the current window
OpenForm	Opens the Servicing Form

3. Save the macro as **Testmacro** and close it.

4. Create another new macro with a first action of **PrintOut** and a second action of **Close**. Enter the **PrintOut** action arguments as shown below.

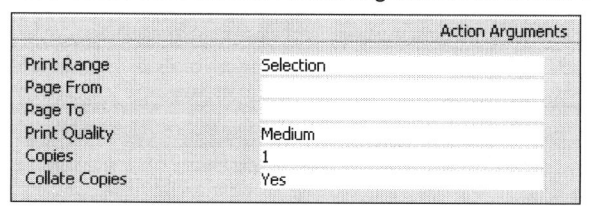

Action Arguments	
Print Range	Selection
Page From	
Page To	
Print Quality	Medium
Copies	1
Collate Copies	Yes

   The **Selection** argument means that only the selected record will be printed.

5. Set the **Save** argument for the **Close** action to **No**. Save the macro as **Printmacro** and close it.

6. Open the **Buses** form in **Design View**. Ensure the **Toolbox** is visible and the **Control Wizards** button is turned off.

7. Create a **Command Button**, at the left of the form in the **Form Footer**.

Driving Lesson 78 - Continued

8. With the **Command Button** selected, view its **Properties**.

9. Select the **Event** tab and click in **On Click** from the property list, i.e. a single click on this button will run the macro.

10. To select which macro to run click the down arrow - a list of available macros is shown.

11. Choose the **Testmacro** macro.

12. Select the **Format** tab and in **Caption**, enter **Service**. This will appear on the button.

13. Macros can be attached to other controls on the form. Click on the image in the centre of the page and view its **Properties** dialog box. Select the **Event** tab.

14. Click in **On Dbl Click** from the property list, i.e. a double click on this object will be needed to run the macro.

15. Click the down arrow and choose the **Printmacro** macro.

16. Click in the **Size** control and view its **Properties**. Select the **Event** tab.

17. Click in **On Key Press** from the property list, i.e. any key press in this field will run the macro.

18. Click the down arrow and choose the **Testmacro** macro.

19. Close the **Properties** dialog box. Save the form.

20. Switch to **Form View** and click the **Service** button on the form. The **Testmacro** macro runs. The form is closed and the **Servicing** form opens.

21. Close the **Servicing** form and open the **Buses** form in **Form View**.

22. Move to record 3 and double click the central image. The macro **Printmacro** runs. The record is printed and the form closes.

23. Open the **Buses** form and click in the **Size** field.

24. Press any character key on the keyboard. The **Testmacro** macro runs. The form is closed and the **Servicing** form opens.

25. Close the **Servicing** form and leave the **Transport** database open.

Driving Lesson 79 - Attaching a Macro to an Object

🅿 Park and Read

Macros can also be assigned to a database object such as a whole form.

👉 Manoeuvres

1. In the **Transport** database, open the **Buses** form in **Design View**.
2. Click on the button in the top left to select the whole form.

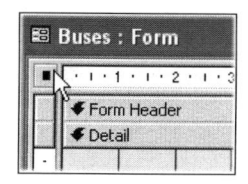

3. Display the **Properties** dialog box and select the **Event** tab. Notice there are many more possible events associated with the form.

4. Click in **On Close** from the property list, i.e. the macro will be triggered when the form is closed.

5. Click the down arrow and choose the **OpenServicing** macro.

6. Close the **Properties** dialog box. Save the form.

7. Switch to **Form View**. Navigate through a few records and then close the form. The **OpenServicing** macro runs and the **Servicing** form opens in maximised format.

8. Close the **Servicing** form and open the **Buses** form in **Design View**.

9. Remove the **OpenServicing** macro from the **On Close** event for the form.

10. Save and close the **Buses** form but leave the database open.

Driving Lesson 80 - Create Macros from Controls

Park and Read

Instead of creating the macro then attaching it to a control, it is possible to create the macro as the control itself is being added to the form (or report). As before, the control can be a button, a field or the form itself. The created macro can be saved as a separate object or embedded with the form. The **Find** macro, which is created here, uses the **Find and Replace** function to search for records using the field specified in the **Action Argument** for the command.

Manoeuvres

1. From the **Transport** database, open the **Buses** form in **Design View**.

2. Ensure the **Control Wizards** button is turned off. Create a **Command Button** at the right of the form in the **Form Footer**.

3. View the **Properties** of the command button. Select the **Event** tab and click in **On Click**.

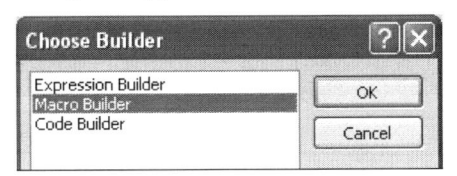

4. Instead of selecting an existing macro, click on the **Build** button, [...]. The **Choose Builder** dialog box appears. Select **Macro Builder**.

5. Click **OK**. At the **Save As** dialog box enter **Find record**. Click **OK**.

6. The **Macro Window** appears. Select the **GoToControl Action** and in the **Action Arguments**, enter **Fleet Number** as the **Control Name**, because this is the field that will be searched during the **Find and Replace** process.

7. On the next **Action** line, choose the **RunCommand Action** and from the **Action Arguments** click in **Command** and select **Find**. This will run the **Find and Replace** command.

Driving Lesson 80 - Continued

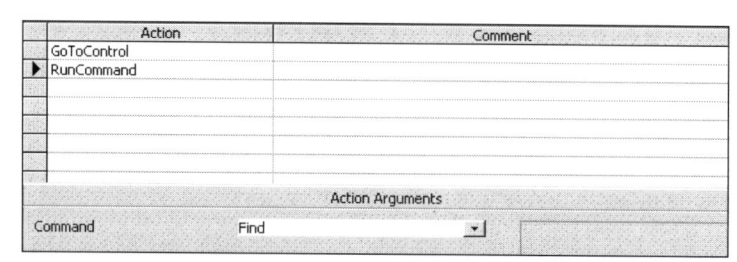

Action	Comment
GoToControl	
RunCommand	

Action Arguments

Command	Find

8. Close the macro, clicking **Yes** to save the changes. The macro now appears in the **On Click** property, `On Click ............ Find record`.

9. On the **Format** tab, change the **Caption** to **Find**. This will appear on the command button.

10. Close the **Properties**, save the form and switch to **Form View**.

11. Click the **Find** button. The **Find and Replace** dialog box appears. Enter the fleet number **L12** in **Find What**.

12. Click **Find Next**. The first matching record appears. What is the driver's first name? Move the dialog box if necessary to see the form.

See the **Answers** section at the back of the guide.

13. Close the **Find** dialog box.

14. Close the form and leave the database open.

… Access 2003

Driving Lesson 81 - Command Button Macros

Park and Read

Macros can be added easily when creating command buttons using the wizard.

Manoeuvres

1. From the **Transport** database, open the **Buses** form in **Design View**.
2. Make sure that **Control Wizards** is switched on, then create a command button in the centre of the **Form Footer**.
3. Select **Miscellaneous** from the list of **Categories** list and **Run Macro** from the list of **Actions**.

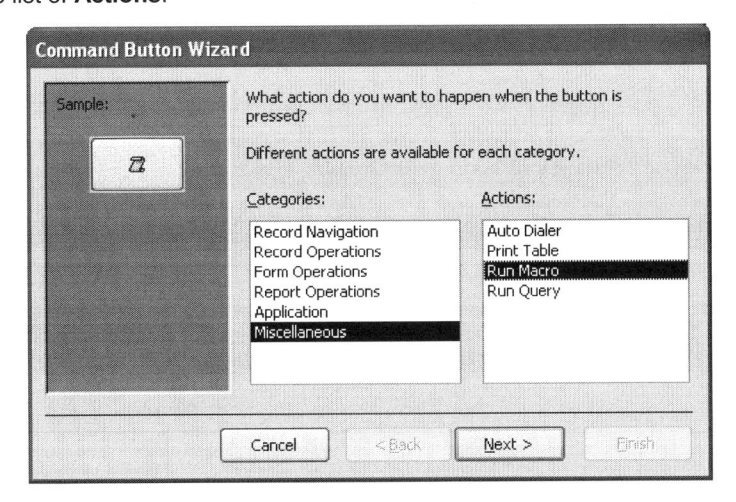

4. Click **Next**. Select **Printmacro** from the list and click **Next** again.
5. Select the **Text** option and type **Print Record** as the text to appear on the button.

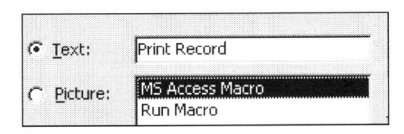

6. Click **Next**. Leave the name unchanged and click **Finish**.
7. Save the form and switch to **Form View**.
8. Click the **Print Record** button to print out a copy of the current record.
9. Close the **Transport** database.

Driving Lesson 82 - Revision

This is not an ECDL test. Testing may only be carried out through certified ECDL test centres. This covers the features introduced in this section. Try not to refer to the preceding Driving Lessons while completing it.

1. Open the **Staff** database.

2. Create a macro to open the **Staff List** table (use the **OpenTable** action) in **Datasheet View**.

3. Add a second action to **Maximize** the display.

4. Save the macro as **ShowStaff** and close it.

5. Create another macro to print the currently selected record and then to close the form.

6. Save the macro as **Printrecord** and close it.

7. Open the **Staff Info** form in **Design View** and select the **Employee No** control. Attach the **Show Staff** macro to this control so that it is activated when the control is double clicked.

8. Create a **Command Button** in the lower part of the **Detail** area. Attach the macro **Printrecord** to the button. Change the button caption to **Print this Record**.

9. Save the form, switch to **Form View** and double click in **Employee No**.

10. Close the **Staff List** table when it opens.

11. Click the **Print this Record** button to print the record and close the form.

12. Close the database.

If you experienced any difficulty completing the Revision, refer back to the Driving Lessons in this section. Then redo the Revision.

Driving Lesson 83 - Revision

This is not an ECDL test. Testing may only be carried out through certified ECDL test centres. This covers the features introduced in this section. Try not to refer to the preceding Driving Lessons while completing it.

1. Open the database **Supermarket** and the **Delete Stock** form in **Design View**.
2. Create a command button in the form footer.
3. View the properties for the button and on the **Format** tab, change the **Caption** to **Delete Record**.
4. Select the **Event** tab and the **On Click** property and then click the **Build** button.
5. Choose the **Macro Builder**.
6. Save the macro as **DeleteRecord**.
7. Set the first **Action** as **MsgBox** and the **Action Arguments** message as **Are you sure you want to delete this record?**
8. Make sure **Beep** is set to **Yes**.
9. From **Type**, select **Warning?**
10. In **Title**, enter **Delete Record**.
11. On the next **Action** line, select the **Action RunCommand** and in **Action Arguments** choose the **DeleteRecord** command.
12. Save and close the macro and close the **Properties** box.
13. Switch to **Form View** and move to record **15**.
14. Test the button. Click **OK** when the **Delete Record** message appears and click **Yes** at the next prompt.
15. Close the form and the database, saving any changes.

If you experienced any difficulty completing the Revision, refer back to the Driving Lessons in this section. Then redo the Revision.

Answers

Driving Lesson 6

Step 7   Data is retrieved from 4 tables.

Driving Lesson 16

Step 7   £57,285.71

Step 9   £104,525.00

Driving Lesson 17

Step 3

Location	MaxOfPrice	MinOfPrice
Central Area	£300,000.00	£56,000.00
DockLand	£120,000.00	£38,000.00
Enterprise Centre	£200,000.00	£45,000.00
Industrial Park	£176,000.00	£34,000.00
Riverside Complex	£250,000.00	£43,000.00
Valley Grove	£150,000.00	£44,000.00

Step 7

Location	Price	Address
Industrial Park	£34,000.00	Unit 2 Boreham Close
DockLand	£38,000.00	17 The Port Buildings
Riverside Complex	£43,000.00	6 Shore Road
Valley Grove	£44,000.00	Unit 68
Enterprise Centre	£45,000.00	17 Cider Place

Step 9

Location	Price	Address
Central Area	£300,000.00	Raby Exhibition Hall
Riverside Complex	£250,000.00	Jupiter Suite
Central Area	£250,000.00	5th Floor, Stanton Tower
Enterprise Centre	£200,000.00	Unit D, Main Building
Central Area	£200,000.00	15 Lothian Enterprise Building
Industrial Park	£176,000.00	7 Elm Court
Enterprise Centre	£175,000.00	86 Kingsway
Central Area	£156,000.00	17 Hartson Chambers
Valley Grove	£150,000.00	12 Desert Road
Riverside Complex	£150,000.00	Suite A, The Marina

Driving Lesson 21

Step 2   There are 6 different engineers.

Step 3   Minimum price £26, maximum price £390.

Step 4   Total price £2550.

Step 5   Keith (£243.00)

Step 8   Keith has 3 jobs over £100.

Step 12   **Like "?#5".** 6 records are found.

Driving Lesson 22

Step 3   Apartment.

Step 7   32a Stanton Tower.

Step 9   8 Sunset Avenue.

Driving Lesson 31

Step 6   3.

Step 7   Because there are records for **JT** on the **Meetings** table and **Cascade** has not been specified.

Step 9   Yes, the **Meetings** table is automatically updated.

Step 10   Because there is no related record with a key of **AS** on **People**.

Driving Lesson 32

Step 6

First Name	Personal records.Surname	Personally referred by
Harry	Hill	Ball
Beryl	Barrington	Ball
Cheryl	Cannock	Barrington

Step 11   4 introductions.

Step 13   10 records

Driving Lesson 37

Step 8   Sandstone Computers shows one record per computer, with repairs shown in a subform. Multitable shows one record for each computer/repair combination.

Driving Lesson 65

Step 6   Three columns in the spreadsheet have the title **Film**. *Access* cannot have duplicate field names so only the first one can be used.

Driving Lesson 66

Step 3   Original total £283,835.

Step 6   New total £291,835.

Driving Lesson 70

Step 7   The original prices were £4, £150, £10, £20 and £14.

Step 8   After running the query they are £4, £165, £11, £22 and £15.40.

Step 11   After modifying they are £4, £173.25, £11.55, £23.10 and £16.17.

Driving Lesson 72

Step 13   Northern Region contains the highest sales figure.

Step 14   Black.

Driving Lesson 80

Step 12   Driver's first name is Gordon.

Glossary

Bound Control	Refers to a field on a form or report that obtains its content from a specific data field on a table.
Field Properties	Define how data is entered and stored in a table.
Foreign Key	A primary key from table A, which is also used as a key field in table B is called a foreign key.
Joins	Define how relationships between tables are applied in queries.
Lookup Field	A field that can obtain (look up) its values from an existing source, either from a built in list or from another table.
Macro	An automated way of performing one or a series of actions.
One-to-many	Any one record from table A may be related to one or many records from table B.
One-to-one	One record from table A is related to one record from table B.
Parameter	A value which is used in an operation, e.g. as a query selection criteria, but can be changed each time the operation is run.
Primary Key	A field which uniquely identifies a record, e.g. telephone number in a table.
Referential Integrity	A set of rules which are applied to a relationship, to prevent or control the alteration and deletion of records in one table, that would affect records in the second table. Ensures the data in related tables is always valid.
Relationships	The ability to connect tables of data, so that no data need to be repeated.
Select Query	The basic type of query, which selects data from one or more tables.
Subdatasheet	A datasheet within a main datasheet which shows details of records from a related, subsidiary table.
Subform	A form within a main form which shows details of records from a related, subsidiary table.
Summary Calculations	In queries, these produce data calculated from a group of records without showing the individual records.
Unbound Control	Refers to a field on a form or report where the content is not from a specific data field on a table, e.g. a label.
Validation Rules	Defines the values which can be entered into a field. Entries that do not conform to the rule cannot be entered.
Wildcards	Characters which represent other unknown characters when selecting records in a query or find operation.

Index

Action Queries 118
   Append 119
   Delete 121
   Make-Table 122
   Update 124

Append Query 119

Average Values 32

Calculated Fields
   In Forms 73
   In Queries 34
   In Reports 99
   Percentages 102

Cascade Options
   Relationships 57

Check Boxes 85

Combo Box
   Manual 81
   Wizard 75-80

Count 31

Crosstab Query 128

Database
   Concepts 9
   Create New 12
   Development 10
   Models 9

Default Values 20

Delete Query 121

Design Table 13

Field Properties 16
   Default Values 20
   Input Masks 25
   Lookup Fields 17
   Mandatory Fields 21
   Validation Rules 23

Find Duplicates Query 130

Find Unmatched Query 131

Form Headers and Footers 88

Forms 61
   Linking 68
   Main/SubForm Manual 66
   Main/Subform Form Wizard 62
   Main/Subform Subform Wizard 64

Form Controls 72
   Calculated Fields 73
   Check Boxes 85
   Combo Box Manual 81
   Combo Box Wizards 75-80
   Command Button Wizard 89
   Form Headers and Footers 88
   Limit to List 78
   List Boxes 83
   Option Groups 86
   Tab Order 77

Group By Queries 30-33

Grouped Reports
   Manual 95
   Wizard 93

Importing Data
   Spreadsheets 109
   Tables 113
   Text Files 111

Input Masks 25

Joins 43
   Self 53

Limit to List 78

Linking Data 114

List Boxes 83

Lookup Fields
   Form 75-81
   Table 17, 19

Macros
   Attach to a Control 136
   Attach to an Object 138
   Command Button 141
   Create from Controls 139
   Create New 134
   Macro Actions 134

Make-Table Query 122

Mandatory Fields 21

Maximum Values 33

Minimum Values 33

Option Groups 86

Parameter Queries 36

Primary Keys 42

Printing
  Reports 105

Properties, Field 16

Queries
  Append 119
  Calculated Fields 34
  Crosstab 128
  Delete 121
  Find Duplicates 130
  Find Unmatched 131
  Group By 30-33
  Make-Table 122
  Parameter 36
  Update 124

Referential Integrity 55

Relationships 41
  Applying 44
  Cascade Options 57
  Joins 51-53
  Many-to-Many 49
  One-to-One 47
  Primary Keys 42
  Referential Integrity 55
  Subdatasheets 48

Reports 92
  Calculated Fields 99
  Calculating Percentages 102
  Grouped Reports Manual 95
  Grouped Reports Wizard 93
  Printing 105
  Report Headers and Footers 103
  Subreports 97

Revision
  Action Queries 125-126
  Field Properties 28
  Forms 70-71
  Fundamentals 15
  Import and Link Data 116-117
  Macros 142-143
  Queries 39-40
  Query Wizards 132
  Relationships 59-60
  Reports 106-107

Self Joins 53

SQL 11

Subdatasheets
  Viewing 48

Subforms 62-67

Subreports 97

Sum 30

Tab Order 77

Table
  Design 13

Update Query 124

Validation Rules 23

Wizards
  Combo Box 75-80
  Command Button 89
  Crosstab Query 128
  Form Wizard 62
  Grouped Report 93
  Subform Wizard 64
  Subreport Wizard 97

Wildcards
  In Queries 38

Record of Achievement Matrix

This Matrix is to be used to measure your progress while working through the guide. This is a learning reinforcement process, you judge when you are competent.

Tick boxes are provided for each feature. 1 is for no knowledge, 2 some knowledge and 3 is for competent. A section is only complete when column 3 is completed for all parts of the section.

For details on sitting ECDL Examinations in your country please contact the local ECDL Licensee or visit the European Computer Driving Licence Foundation Limited web site at http://www.ecdl.org.

ECDL/ICDL Module AM5 - Database Advanced Level

Tick the Relevant Boxes **1**: No Knowledge   **2**: Some Knowledge   **3**: Competent

Section	No.	Driving Lesson	1	2	3
1 Fundamentals	1	Database Concepts			
	2	Database Development			
	3	SQL			
	4	Creating a Database			
	5	Creating Tables			
2 Field Properties	7	Lookup Fields			
	8	Lookup a Table			
	9	Default Values			
	10	Setting a Mandatory Field			
	11	Validation Rules/Text			
	12	Input Masks			
3 Queries	14	Sum			
	15	Count			
	16	Average Values			
	17	Maximum and Minimum Values			
	18	Calculated Fields in Queries			
	19	Parameter Queries			
	20	Using Wildcards in Queries			
4 Relationships	23	Applying a Primary Key			
	24	Applying Relationships			
	26	One-to-One Relationships			
	26	Many-to-Many Relationships			
	27	Applying Joins			
	28	Self Joins			
	29	Referential Integrity			
	30	Cascade Options			
5 Forms	33	Main/Subform: Form Wizard			
	34	Main/Subform: Subform Wizard			
	35	Main/Subform: Manual			
	36	Linking Forms			
6 Form Controls	39	Calculated Fields in Forms			
	40	Combo Box 1: Wizard			
	41	Limit to List			
	42	Combo Box 2: Wizard			
	43	Combo Box 3: Wizard			
	44	Combo Box: Manual			
	45	List Boxes			

ECDL/ICDL Module AM5 - Database Advanced Level

Tick the Relevant Boxes **1**: No Knowledge   **2**: Some Knowledge   **3**: Competent

Section	No.	Driving Lesson	1	2	3
6 Form Controls - Continued	46	Check Boxes			
	47	Option Groups			
	48	Form Headers and Footers			
	49	Command Button: Wizard			
7 Reports	52	Grouped Report: Wizard			
	53	Grouped Report: Manual			
	54	Subreports			
	55	Calculated Fields in Reports			
	56	Calculating Percentages			
	57	Report Headers and Footers			
	58	Printing Reports			
8 Import and Link Data	61	Importing Spreadsheets			
	62	Importing Text Files			
	63	Importing Tables			
	64	Linking Data			
9 Action Queries	67	Append Query			
	68	Delete Query			
	69	Make-Table Query			
	70	Update Query			
10 Query Wizards	73	Crosstab Query			
	74	Find Duplicates Query			
	75	Find Unmatched Query			
11 Macros	77	Create a New Macro			
	78	Attaching a Macro to a Control			
	79	Attaching a Macro to an Object			
	80	Create Macros from Controls			
	81	Command Button Macros			

Other Products from CiA Training Ltd

CiA Training Ltd is a leading publishing company, which has consistently delivered the highest quality products since 1985. A wide range of flexible and easy to use self teach resources has been developed by CiA's experienced publishing team to aid the learning process. These include the following ECDL Foundation approved products at the time of publication of this product:

- ECDL/ICDL Syllabus 5.0

- ECDL/ICDL Advanced Syllabus 2.0

- ECDL/ICDL Revision Series

- ECDL/ICDL Advanced Syllabus 2.0 Revision Series

- e-Citizen

Previous syllabus versions also available - contact us for further details.

We hope you have enjoyed using our materials and would love to hear your opinions about them. If you'd like to give us some feedback, please go to:

www.ciatraining.co.uk/feedback.php

and let us know what you think.

New products are constantly being developed. For up to the minute information on our products, to view our full range, to find out more, or to be added to our mailing list, visit:

www.ciatraining.co.uk